ELTON JOHN

DICK TATHAM &
TONY JASPER

octopus
in association with
Phoebus

CONTENTS

FOREWORD

In crowd-drawing terms few on the contemporary music scene can compete with Elton John. He has filled the largest stadiums in the world, like the 100,000 Wembley Stadium in London and the Dodger Stadium in L.A. No one since the Beatles has played at the Dodger Stadium with such outstanding success.

Almost all the Elton John albums have been sensational smash hits and their total sales exceed 25,000,000. Television companies all over the world queue up for his time. He is a superstar.

It is possible that there may be greater stars than Elton John, but they will be nothing less than breathtaking for that's the order of the Elton John performance. Long may it continue.

Elton

First published 1976 by
Octopus Books Limited,
59 Grosvenor Street, London W.1.

ISBN 0 7064 0548 X

©1975/1976 Phoebus Publishing Company/BPC Publishing Limited.
This book has been produced by Phoebus Publishing Company
in co-operation with Octopus Books Limited.

Produced by Mandarin Publishers Limited,
22a Westlands Road, Quarry Bay, Hong Kong.
Printed in Hong Kong.

Redferns

INTRODUCTION

He erupts on stage amid a shower of glitter. The sparse hair is bright with whatever color he thought of last. With the ritzy glasses and in his gaudy, utterly fantastic clothes he might well be mistaken for an envoy from outer space.

In a trice he's rocking on — jubilantly, potently, deafeningly, clearly enjoying it all as much as the crowd. Which is plenty. Throughout his show he whips his audience into one wild frenzy after another — firing them with his pulsing, buoyant, splendidly exciting music and by an uninhibited showmanship true to the highest traditions of showbiz.

Elton Hercules John — the larger-than-life entertainer who, as the world knows, has fashioned an incredible, million-dollar mix of rock and vaudeville.

Once he was simply Reginald Kenneth Dwight — former fat boy from Pinner, England — who was fettered by his fatness and parental disciplines. Now he is making it up to himself, in public and in no uncertain manner.

He's been compared to Liberace, and that figures. He resembles him in knowing what showmanship is all about and in his ready flair for sending himself up. But his private self is in stark contrast to his public ego — so that he is sensible, quiet, modest, friendly and never in the least danger of taking himself too seriously. As a person, Elton is far removed from a rock type. He shuns rock slang, he wears his hair short, he doesn't take drugs. And he reveres such pinnacles of showbiz as Katharine Hepburn, Groucho Marx, Marlene Dietrich and Mae West.

He is a one man music spectacle. Not for him the concert atmosphere of a solitary spotlight on an earnest piano player with the audience steeped in reverential silence. When he wants a show to explode, it explodes! He is prepared to consider every possible kind of special effect in order to create a spectacular mood.

A stuntman doubling for him may glide onto the stage from a downward sloping trapeze wire. Or Elton may appear flanked by Playboy Bunnies. Or the curtain may rise to reveal Elton seated at a piano from which clouds of dry ice are billowing. Or a barrage of white doves may be released from a battery of grand pianos. And that's only a start!

Once the show is moving, the sheer entertainment of the performing personality that is Elton John takes over. His energy is truly remarkable. Pausing only to wipe his forehead, or take a drink, he wastes the minimum amount of time between numbers. He radiates infectious enjoyment, both to the other members of the band and to the swaying, singing, stomping audience.

The pace and variety of the show may exhaust Elton but they drain the audience as well. At the end the prostrate bodies of overwhelmed fans can resemble the last act of Hamlet. Which isn't bad for someone who's not even a sex symbol!

He has the most unlikely looks for a rock star. He is balding and has been fat for most of his career. He stands a modest 5ft. 7ins. and has poor sight. His looks are, at the most, pleasant and average. It is a sign of his moral courage that he never allowed this to deter him from pressing ahead with the traditionally tough struggle to get established.

Tubby Little Singer

Clearly he's never given a damn for his physical shortcomings. He wears no wig or contact lenses and only increases his height with grossly-platformed boots because they look ridiculous.

"I'm a tubby little singer," he once said, "and can't understand why people scream for me. There must be a reason but God knows what it is." One reason could be that he works prodigiously. His show may last two hours or more but he doesn't spare himself for a second.

"I can't understand those people who say they don't like doing concerts," he once declared in Dallas. "It's the greatest thing in the world to stand on a stage and see people in the front rows smiling and know they have come to see you.

"The stage, in reality, is the closest you can ever get to most of the fans. They may say hello backstage or in a hotel or something, but even that is not as close as seeing a show and being affected by the music. That's why I get upset if I play badly. Not only for me, but because I know I've disappointed the audience." Nor does he lament the traveling, the way many rock stars do. He says he actually likes it.

Next to his performing, the most potent part of his appeal is probably his attitude to life: it mustn't be taken too seriously and must be enjoyed to the full. He has, of course, the wealth to do this in the grand manner and to indulge in such flamboyant whims as flying a Chinese chef from Los Angeles to Britain to cook his Christmas dinner. Millions of fans enjoy his lavish lifestyle by proxy and respect him for having won it by talent and toil. He is, after all, a superstar.

THE ELTON JOHN STORY

Elton's story starts with the birth of Reginald Kenneth Dwight on March 25, 1947, in Pinner, Middlesex, on the outskirts of London. He was the only child of Stanley and Sheila Dwight. Stanley was a squadron leader in the Royal Air Force who also had many years' experience as a professional trumpeter.

Music entered young Reg's life early. His mother recalls that when he was only three they tried to cool his irritable moods by seating him at the piano and letting him bang away. But the banging soon took a tuneful form and the Dwights realized there was a prodigy in the home.

"We sent Elton for lessons when he was four," Mrs Dwight says. "We used to let him sleep during the day so that he could play for our friends at evening parties." Elton recalls his parents had a stack of 78s by such stars of the early '50s as Rosemary Clooney, Frankie Laine, Guy Mitchell, Kay Starr and Billy May.

"When I was four," he says, "I had a mass of bubbly hair. I looked like Shirley Temple. My piano idols were Charlie Kunz, who'd been famous in Britain for years, and Winifred Atwell — the West Indian who'd settled in Britain and was great at playing anything from the classics to pop. 'The Skater's Waltz' became my first main party piece."

The lad plodded on with his conventional training — becoming good enough to play at his school's morning assembly at a tender age but, when he was nine, his musical outlook was suddenly set alight.

"My mother came home one afternoon with two discs. She said she had never heard anything like them and thought they were fantastic. When I heard them, I agreed. They were Elvis's 'Heartbreak Hotel' and Bill Haley's 'ABC Boogie.' They were the first big influences in my life, I loved banging away at those two numbers on piano. It was in a magazine in a barber's shop that I first read about Elvis and the way he performed. It seemed incredible. Then I saved my pocket money and bought Little Richard's 'She's Got It' and 'The Girl Can't Help It.'

"My mother liked some rock but not Little Richard and she wouldn't let me play his stuff. I was really angry because his was my favourite disc. Pop music became my whole life and my aim was to be a pop star or at least something to do with the business — even if it was only selling discs in a shop."

While his mother influenced him positively in his ambition, his father's attitude was rather negative. Elton was once quoted as saying, "I was always frightened of my dad." So perhaps this wanting to be a star also has something to do with wanting to prove himself. "Father didn't want me to be a rock star," he recalls, "he wanted me to get a decent job with British European Airways or something. Father only liked me playing classical things. The Air Force does tend to breed snobbery and my father was a bit of a snob." This barrier was removed by his parents' divorce when he was a schoolboy. "After the divorce," he says, "I had more freedom. My mother always encouraged me to play whatever kind of music I liked."

First Group

Elton's first public appearance was at a local music festival when he was 12, in which he played classical pieces. Around the same time, he won a scholarship which entitled him to Saturday morning lessons at the Royal Academy of Music in London. He kept them up for five years — though he admits he sometimes gave the lessons a miss in order to play soccer. Only a year or so after starting the lessons, Elton formed his first group. They were called the Corvettes — after a shaving lotion.

"I met this guy Stuart Brown, a friend of my cousin, who played guitar. I was very fat and when I said I played piano he laughed helplessly. So I showed him. I did my Jerry Lee Lewis bit and he stopped laughing. We got a band together and played at Scout huts and the like. We had no amplifiers. It was just a hobby and faded out after a few months.

"Two years later I talked myself into a job at a local pub. I sang and played — mainly Jim Reeves's numbers — every Friday, Saturday and Sunday. They paid a small wage and let me take a box round. The customers were kind and soon I had enough to buy an electric piano. Then I ran into Stuart again and he suggested starting another band." Elton was, predictably, enthusiastic. "We started with a four-piece and then we decided to add brass so we put an ad. in a paper and got a tenor sax player and trumpeter who were much better musicians than the rest of us."

Elton was already wearing spectacles — though originally bad sight hadn't been the cause. "I began wearing glasses when I was 13 to copy Buddy Holly," he says. "After 18

A nine-year-old musical prodigy, reveling in rock & roll.

months I found I couldn't see without them. If any young fans are thinking of copying me, I advise them to forget it."

Elton was attending Pinner County Grammar School, but only three weeks before his final exams, he left. His cousin Roy Dwight, a professional soccer player, had happened to hear that Mills Music — a publishing firm in London's Tin Pan Alley — wanted a junior. "I landed the job, which consisted of running errands, making tea, parceling sheet music and so on. I was bored with school and happy to leave and though my music teacher protested at my decision, I did what I wanted. Mills paid me about £4.50 ($12) a week.

"In the evenings I played with the band, which we had called Bluesology — after a disc by French guitarist Django Reinhardt. An agent saw the band and asked if we'd be interested in backing American stars on tour in Britain. This was a major step forward for so inexperienced a band, but the job wasn't without its problems. First we auditioned for Wilson Pickett but the guitarist he'd brought from the States couldn't stand our drummer. Then we were taken on to back Major Lance, which was when I quit my job at Mills.

Unwanted Singer

"I looked incredible at this time. A fatty with glasses and with a terrible inferiority complex about my appearance, which it took me years to lose. After Major Lance we backed Patti LaBelle — who also didn't like our drummer — Doris Troy, the Inkspots (which was a bit of a fiasco) and Billy Stewart. Billy was way above the others. He would play three or four gigs a night and take it in his stride." Elton by then had become very fond of soul music — buying all the Stax and Motown discs he could find. "I was a soul freak," he recalls, "and snobbish about it."

Bluesology gained some minor success, performing extensively on the Continent and in Britain. They were due to tour Sweden when they met Long John Baldry in the Cromwellian, one of London's most popular clubs with the rock crowd. John, an experienced bluesman, was looking for a group and asked them to join him. They agreed on the understanding they could start after they had played three weeks of dates in Sweden, to which they were already committed.

Elton had for some time been the unwanted singer. At the start of Bluesology he had done a few vocals only to be crowded out by Stuart Brown, who had regarded himself as the singer in the band and much the same happened after Bluesology had joined forces with Baldry, early in 1967.

"Elton was a great little guy," Long John later recalled. "He was taking pills to get thin and though they worked, they also tended to make him aggressive and short-tempered. He shouted a lot, which I found amusing. He wanted to sing very much, but there were a couple of other singers in the band apart from me and although I would have let him sing I allowed myself to be overruled.

"He was already writing songs at the time but they were hackneyed and nothing like those he was to do later. It was not until after he'd left the group and was doing demos that I realized what was going to happen."

Apart from working with Baldry, Bluesology made three discs, which flopped, but in the autumn of 1967 Baldry had a number one chart hit in Britain with "Let The Heartaches Begin." One result was a flood of offers to appear in night clubs, many of which he accepted, and Bluesology went along as the backing band. Elton grew increasingly restless, he didn't like night clubs and he liked the fact that he was doing no singing even less.

In an attempt to further his own career, he auditioned for Liberty Records — the American label which was then setting up its own distribution offices in London. The audition was hardly successful. "Liberty asked me to sing five songs," he recalls. "But all I knew was 'He'll Have To Go' and 'I Love You Because.' I hadn't sung in years and I was awful, they turned me down and I don't blame them."

Teamed with Taupin

Elton had approached Liberty in reply to an advert asking for new talent. A failed audition in 999 cases out of a thousand, leads nowhere. This was the thousandth case. It happened because a lady in Lincolnshire had retrieved from the waste basket a letter which had been written by her son in response to the Liberty ad. and then thrown away in an act of hopelessness. She, having faith in the boy's ability, had posted it on to Liberty.

Her son was 17-year-old Bernie Taupin. He wanted to compose lyrics, and he had already written poems some of which he thought, albeit hesitantly, might be usefully set to music. A man at Liberty named Ray Williams showed Elton a few things Bernie had written because he knew that Elton wanted to get into songwriting but was hopeless at words.

"I was impressed by Bernie's work," Elton recalls. "And I was keen to team up with him, although the way I was

feeling, I'd have been keen to team up with anyone!" He was feeling deeply depressed and it is easy to see why. He had been with Bluesology four years — traveling in scant comfort from one gig to another, earning little, doing no singing and seeing no hope of a break into better things.

Even when he and Baldry had agreed that they would soon part company, Elton had made up his mind that he wouldn't be joining another group. But he had a living to earn and though he met Bernie Taupin and they agreed to work together, the financial prospects for two unknown songwriters were hardly golden. The first John/Taupin songs were published by the Hollies' music company while Elton was still with Bluesology.

Living Wage

Late in 1967 a man came into Elton's life who was to play a vast and decisive part in his future — Dick James — a singer who had turned to music publishing and who had made a fortune from the songs of John Lennon and Paul McCartney. Through a business link between Dick James and the Hollies' company, Elton made demos of songs he had written with Bernie in the four-track studio in Dick James's headquarters. Elton and Bernie didn't know Dick James, but one day James happened to ask about the Reg Dwight who was doing so much work in the studio.

Caleb Quaye, a guitarist and sound engineer who had been helping Elton record the tapes, told James about the young writers and said they were good. James listened, agreed and signed Elton and Bernie to a writing contract and, since he wanted them to aim at the Top 20, he also signed Elton as a singer.

But what sent Elton over the moon was that James offered him a retainer of £10 ($25) a week. It was a tremendous break! "The retainer was enough to live on," says Elton, "and meant that I would be able to leave Bluesology without financial worries. I had become so desperate and miserable in the group that I just had to get out." It was decided to launch Elton as a singer with one of the songs he'd written with Bernie: "I've Been Loving You." The session was produced by Caleb Quaye for Dick James's company and released through the Philips label.

Elton agreed that it was time to change his name. "I realized Reg Dwight was hopeless," he recalls. "It

The galaxy of badges sprinkled on a jacket is tame by later standards.

17

sounded like a library assistant. My last gig with Baldry was in Scotland, Caleb was there and I knew I had to think of another name without delay. One of the guys in Bluesology was Elton Dean; I figured I could take part of his name but not all of it, or he'd kick up. People started firing off short names and when someone said John I settled for that.

"Becoming Elton John did me good personally. I'd had a terrible inferiority complex as Reg Dwight and the name change helped me get out of it. Later I thought of changing it again but no one could come up with anything better."

"I've Been Loving You" was released on March 1, 1968. It sank without trace. More hopeful was the result of Dick James's submission of a John/Taupin song as a possible British entry for the 1968 Eurovision Song Contest. It had reached the shortlist of six, from which the final song was selected by votes from TV viewers.

Elton went on to complete an album of songs he'd written with Bernie but Dick James decided it wouldn't sell and it wasn't released. Nearly three years later he was to say, "I played that first album again the other night. When it was made, I had thought it great. Now it was so embarrassing." Elton earned money by making demos of other people's songs and doing back-up vocal work at recording sessions. He recalls the special kindness of Roger Cook and Roger Greenaway — an established singing/writing duo also known as David and Jonathan. They encouraged Elton and

Below: Bernie Taupin, early days in a songwriting partnership.

Bernie in their writing, gave Elton a lot of session work and when Roger Cook made his first solo disc he chose the John/Taupin "Skyline Pigeon" — released in August, 1968.

Unfortunately several other singers also recorded this beautiful song and split the sales so that no one had a hit with it. In the meantime, Elton was making cover versions of hits for a chain store label, singing in the style of Stevie Wonder and other stars.

In mid-1968 a second man appeared whose influence was to be vital. He was Steve Brown who had recently arrived at Dick James Music from EMI Records to work as a song plugger. A former musician, he had played baritone sax with Emile Ford and the Checkmates, a hit group in Britain some years before.

"When Steve Brown arrived," Elton said later, "he told us our songs weren't good and that we should write the way we felt rather than with the charts in mind. That was very courageous as he was just a plugger. But we were desperate for help and from then on we wrote for ourselves. It was a battle with Dick at first because he thought we should be writing Top 20 stuff, but Steve gradually won him over."

Cool Candor

However, having agreed to the new approach, Dick James went all the way, agreeing to Steve's request to produce Elton's next single, "Lady Samantha," even though he had never produced before. "We spent one evening on 'Lady Samantha,'" Steve was to recall. "After the session we were all a bit despondent. We thought it probably shouldn't be released. But within the next ten days, everyone started getting enthusiastic."

"Samantha" came out on January 17, 1969. It was both a failure and a success. It was raved over by DJs and gained a lot of airtime but it only sold about 10,000 and didn't make the charts. However, months later in the States it was a track on a million-selling Three Dog Night album which was useful both for royalties and publicity.

Even back in the days of "Lady Samantha," Elton was refreshing in his views. "He is very adamant," said his record company publicity handout, "about how much talent he and other pop writers have and about how seriously they should take themselves." And they quoted him as saying: "A lot of writers think their stuff is poetry and treat it as such. Just a few are justified, but the majority are kidding themselves and it's sad." He was equally candid about his own career: "I'm glad things haven't gone too smoothly. If I had had a hit straight after leaving

the group, I'd be unbearable now. As it is, having to work for success is bringing valuable experience. I get one hell of a kick just from hearing one of our songs on radio and that's the way it should be."

Steve Brown went on to produce Elton's first album release: "Empty Sky" and also another single "It's Me That You Need," which flopped. He then asked to be replaced, modestly feeling some other producer might be better for Elton. However, he continued to be closely linked with Elton's career — being given the album credit of "co-ordinator" — and was active in bringing in two men whose work on Elton's discs was to be outstanding.

Elton and Bernie had a mass of material ready but when several established producers were approached, they all said that they were too busy to help in the near future. The first man Brown brought in was an arranger, Paul Buckmaster, who was also a classical composer, pop composer and cellist. He had been arranger on the David Bowie hit "Space Oddity" and he had also just had a hit of his own. In partnership with organist Tim Mycroft, and using the name Sounds Nice, he had made the charts with the instrumental "Love At First Sight."

Elton and Bernie went to see Paul. They played him some of their songs, he played them some of his recordings and they agreed to work together. Paul was then asked about a producer and suggested Gus Dudgeon. He had produced "Space Oddity" and "Love At First Sight" and had worked successfully with a number of British groups. Steve took some John/Taupin songs to Gus who liked them and, after a certain amount of persuasion, agreed to produce Elton.

Rebellious Costumes

The new album was started early in 1970. Dick James had said he wanted the finest results possible, no matter the cost. The first track put down was "Take Me To The Pilot," and Elton recalls that "things clicked into place with Gus right away." The album took 55 hours of recording time and cost about £6500 ($16,000). As Dick James later said, it was a lot to spend on a relatively new artist — but everyone concerned felt it was worth it. Like "Empty Sky," the new album "Elton John" was released on Dick James's own label, DJM.

At that time Elton had long hair, a Zapata moustache and was fast developing a taste for bright clothes. A hint of things to come had been evident shortly before the release of "Empty Sky," when he started going around in shirts colorfully adorned by Noddy, a children's fictional character, which had been made from nursery curtain material by a neighbor who ran a boutique. Elton was grateful for the shirts and for the fact that the good lady plastered her boutique walls with posters of him and Bernie.

The clothes were to become a major part of the Elton John image — and for reasons he later traced to his early years. "The clothes thing," he once declared, "is very me, psychologically speaking. Because I was always very fat when I was young, I had to buy clothes which were awful. When you're fat you can't buy nice clothes and today I'm probably rebelling against that.

"To realize I'm a bit crazy, you only have to look at my clothes. Those platform shoes of mine caused a stir. Why did I wear them? Just for a laugh. It gives the audience a giggle and you get a nice atmosphere right from the start. But the real reason goes deeper. Perhaps it started when I was a kid, my dad was strict and I had to wear dull clothes. So as soon as I got the chance, I went to the other extreme. If I'd had more freedom as a kid, I might be wearing smart suits today."

During the summer of 1971 Elton had a suit made by Elvis's tailor. It was of white crepe, hand-embroidered with red and pink roses plus diamanté edging. With it went a Mickey Mouse shirt, wide-brim hat bedecked with stars and frilly Bermuda shorts. But right from the start, Elton looked on his outrageous garb as a big laugh. "I couldn't compete with the Bowies or the Jaggers," he once declared. "I haven't the figure. I'd look like Donald Dumpling. So I try to make people grin. It's probably made people react against me a bit, but that's just the effect I wanted."

Playful Parody

The crucial point is that Elton took his dressing-up to ludicrous lengths in order to ram home the point that he refused to be pretentious about his music. "Here am I," he declared in 1972, "a pudgy little man in outrageous gear leaping at a piano. I don't want to sit there in Levis and a T-shirt because everyone would go serious and say, 'Wow! Great!' My songs aren't that serious and so the way to escape the James Taylor heavy syndrome is to dress up."

"Border Song" — Elton's first single of 1970 — gained critical acclaim and even Dusty Springfield, who had been the dream girl of his early teens, came up to say she thought it a fine song. More plaudits came for the album "Elton John" which was released soon

after and for the single "Rock & Roll Madonna," which appeared in June. Despite the praise lavished on them, none of these made the charts. Dick James, far from deterred, opted for the bold, shrewd stroke of sending Elton on a promotion trip to the States.

Already teamed with Elton were the two musicians who were to form the nucleus of a group: drummer Nigel Olsson and bassman Dee Murray, who had made their stage bow with Elton at London's Roundhouse Theatre that April.

Turn of the Tide

For their September visit to the States, Elton and company arrived in Los Angeles to be greeted by a reception committee including a double-decker London bus to take them on a tour of Beverly Hills and Hollywood. "We were only in the States three weeks but the experience changed our lives," said Elton. The fact was that he and his band were a sensation right from the first show at their first booking: a week at the Los Angeles' Troubadour — the city's very classy rock club. A packed audience greeted them. Word had got around — thanks to imported Elton discs and the Stateside release of the "Elton John" album. The audience had gone to their seats a full hour before the start and in the front row was one of Elton's idols: Leon Russell.

Elton came on in a red T-shirt proclaiming ROCK AND ROLL in white letters. A battery of high-powered speakers surrounded him. He opened with "Your Song," the applause came in a tidal wave and from then on it was victory all the way. Elton John was in orbit in the States!

As one critic declared, "Elton is a giant addition to rock's ever-changing hierarchy." Another wrote: "Elton's style of combining some country music with good ole rock & roll is further enhanced by the melodrama of his falling to his knees to bang away at the piano, which he did to everyone's pleasure on that nasty ole message song 'Burn Down The Mission.' "

Personalities like Randy Newman, the Beach Boys, Quincy Jones and Graham Nash came to see Elton. To critics, fellow performers and the public alike, Elton John had arrived. Not in his own country, where he was still relatively unknown, but in the States, the very mecca of rock music. Ironically, he had conquered the hardest market first.

Elton did 50 supercharged sets in L.A., San Francisco and Philadelphia during those three weeks. He climbed on pianos, he wore black coveralls with

white stars and red coveralls with white stars and aluminum-colored boots with stars imprinted in the leather. He proved without doubt that even in the world of rock there is no business like show business.

Back in Britain, things were starting to move at last and in October, Elton did a smash-hit concert at London's Royal Albert Hall. As one perceptive critic wrote, "Elton is just too much. He brings back the good old days of enthusing audiences. At his grand piano, flicking the tails of his yellow lamé coat over the chair, he has an expression which tells you he desperately wants to laugh. He adopts great rock star poses . . . yet he lets you know he doesn't take the business too seriously."

Professional Appreciation

At about the same time, Elton had also completed his third album, "Tumbleweed Connection," and was in the process of completing the score of the film *Friends*, which he had written with Paul Buckmaster. But the demand for his quick return to the States was powerful and he crossed the Atlantic again in the late October of 1970. As on the first visit, standing ovations greeted him and the stars were eager to make contact.

"We were in New York," says Elton, "when Bernie and I were asked to meet The Band in their hotel, which was just across the road. Bernie was shaken up with nerves but when we met them they were really nice. We talked for about three hours before we had to leave for Philadelphia while they headed in the opposite direction to upstate New York. Our gig in Philly was a wonderful success and when we went back to the dressing room, The Band were there! They had brought their show forward two hours and flown in their private plane to watch our act. They said they hoped we would go to Woodstock some time to record at their place and Robbie Robertson asked us to write a song for them. I think Bernie was embarrassed because Robbie was his idol of the moment."

Inevitably, Elton was breaking through on the U.S. disc scene. The "Elton John" album sold a quarter-million by November and thousands of copies of "Empty Sky" were being imported. Everything pointed towards imminent superstardom. In New York he did a live radio show in eight-track stereo and a performance in Santa Monica was filmed partly for a Henry Mancini spectacular and partly for a half-hour Elton John Show designed for international TV screening.

It was no wonder that British DJs voted Elton "the man who made the most impact in pop during 1970." He himself laughingly declared, "I didn't even want to be a performer. I would have sooner stayed at home writing songs. But I'm having the time of my life!" It was hardly surprising that Elton's American successes soon had repercussions in Britain. Early in 1971 his single "Your Song" rose high in the British charts. In March that year it was estimated that his albums "Elton John" and "Tumbleweed Connection" had sold 1,250,000 copies in the States and Britain and that in the last six months his earnings had topped $600,000.

Elton's mother, a government clerical officer, had been somewhat embarrassed by her son's appearance during the early days of his emergence from obscurity. "I used to be a bit shocked by his clothes," she once declared. "He would wear a big hairy coat, wide-brimmed hat and dark glasses. When he looked like that, I didn't want to be associated with him, I would tell him to walk down the street on his own."

But by 1971, Elton had moved to an apartment in London's affluent West End. "We've helped all we could," said his mother in the October of that year. "It's been our whole life. I did nag him about his clothes and his hair but then I had been living in this suburban place, now I go up to London and meet his friends and he looks fine."

1971 was a very good year for Elton John despite disappointing British sales for the "Madman Across The Water" album. He played many weeks in the States, toured Britain and Australia, had a spate of disc releases and triggered off vast publicity wherever he went. In the spring he had two albums released in Britain at more or less the same time: "17.11.70" from his live radio show and the soundtrack of *Friends* which had already gained him a Gold Record in the States.

Elton Hercules

At the end of '71 Elton bought a luxury home, a split-level bungalow on a private estate which boasted John Lennon and Donovan amongst its residents. He called the house "Hercules," after a track on his coming album, and his first improvements there included doing up the swimming pool, displaying his collection of paintings (for which he'd not had enough wall space in his flat) and installing a large jukebox which he proceeded to stock with current chart hits.

Shortly after his return from the States at the end of 1971 he told his

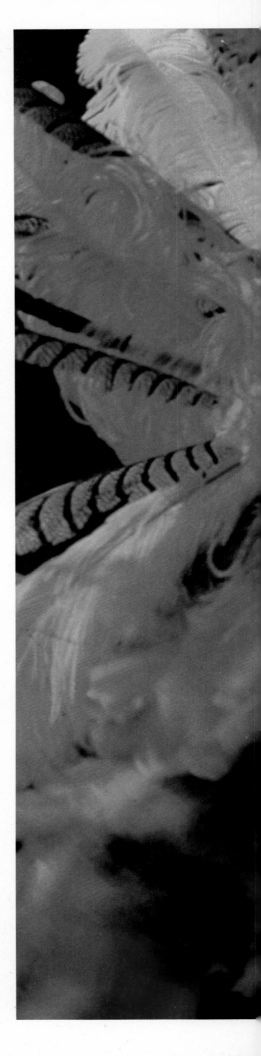

Terry O'Neill

mother that he had legally changed his name to Elton Hercules John. He explained, "I'm fed up with people saying, 'This is Elton John but his real name is Reginald Kenneth Dwight.' Some people might not like calling me Elton, so I picked Hercules as an alternative. You may call me Herk if you like." True to character Elton Hercules intended to enjoy his new-found wealth and fame. He loved to entertain at his home and indulge himself by buying all kinds of luxuries.

Elton's first dinner guests at "Hercules" were fellow star Marc Bolan and wife June. They and other visitors were able to feast their eyes on an impressive array of their host's cars: a Rolls, Daimler, Mercedes, vintage Bentley and Mini GT. A useful addition was a minibike powered by something akin to a lawnmower engine. Elton would often venture forth in the Rolls with the minibike in the back. If, on the outskirts of the city, he got snarled up in traffic, he would park the Rolls in a side street and zip to his destination on the minibike.

Added Impetus

But in the first months of 1972 he was seldom at "Hercules." He was glad that in his absence his mother and stepfather usually moved in. As he had no servants, happily doing cooking, ironing and other chores himself, he knew his home would be well looked after. Also, stepfather Fred (a painter-decorator whom his mother had married some years earlier) was able to wield a professional brush on inside and outside paintwork.

In the late summer of 1971, Elton had announced that his next album would be recorded in France, and in February, 1972, he, Bernie and the group congregated at the Strawberry Studios in the Chateau d'Hèrouville, 30 miles from Paris. It was to be a different sort of album and one of the changes was a new group member.

Just before going to France, Elton had signed the gifted, 20-year-old Scots guitarist Davey Johnstone — who could also play mandolin, sitar, banjo and lute. His arrival was, as Elton had expected, a shot in the arm. After the hectic, punishing schedules of 1971 and the attacks of some musical critics, Elton had become jaded and some-what disillusioned. "Davey," says Elton, "took pressure off the rest of us." Up to that point, guitar had featured little on Elton's discs and its new prominence would facilitate a cut-back in the massed strings of earlier records. Elton's voice and piano would receive greater emphasis. It was more of a rock & roll band which went to

23

France to make Elton's first studio album without an array of session musicians.

"The chateau," says Elton, "had a crumbling splendor and gave us just the atmosphere we wanted. We didn't have to pack everything away at the end of a session and so we could work at night and sleep by day. We had a great little team. Everything was written and recorded very quickly. The album was done in three weeks." The result was "Honky Chateau."

An example of Elton's ready and handsome generosity came in the early part of 1972. Late the previous year, his lawyer had taken him to the new Shaw Theatre in London to see "Good Lads At Heart" — a production by Britain's National Youth Theatre. "The visit turned me on to the theater for the first time," he said later. "I went to the Shaw several times afterwards and was knocked out by its atmosphere and by the efforts of the NYT to provide theater specially for young people." The NYT was seeking financial help at the time and so Elton put on four fund-raising shows at the Shaw — plus a free one for NYT members unable to afford charity prices. His generous efforts raised £3000 ($8,000) for the NYT.

Suspicious Shoes

Early in April, Elton flew to the States for another tour. His airport arrival at Los Angeles had unexpected results when four pairs of his boots and a pair of his shoes came under suspicion because they had heels seven or eight inches high. Customs agents called a shoemaker to examine them, explaining that: "Shoes with secret compartments are often used to smuggle drugs and jewels." Nothing so sinister was found in Elton's footwear, and rather than throw a tantrum, Elton was characteristically good-humored about the incident. "The star," said an official, "was very co-operative."

It happened that one of Elton's gigs was in Houston, Texas and the link between his latest single, "Rocket Man," taken from "Honky Chateau," and the Apollo 16 mission then in progress didn't need to be spelt out in neon signs. He went to the space center to lunch with Al Warden, Apollo 15 module command pilot, and this time Elton was the one asking for a signed photograph. In the course of the visit Elton and his band spent time in one of the grounded space ships and were at the center at the time of the Apollo 16 splashdown.

After another all-systems-go U.S. tour, Elton returned to Britain. Asked to explain how his success in the States had started, he replied, "I realized I had to do more than sit at the piano and sing, so I wore a pink lamé suit and sometimes I put on Mickey Mouse ears. But the real pay-off was when I stood on the piano and wiggled my bum!"

"Honky Chateau" and "Rocket Man" were hits on both sides of the Atlantic, but even as the two records were gathering momentum, Elton and his team were back at the chateau. He had had only a short break in Britain before going to France. He was tired but determined to press on. "We went to the chateau in the June with only one song," Elton said later. "Bernie was in America and his lyrics started coming in by post and I just sat down and wrote the music. I really enjoyed doing this despite being in bad health and on the verge of a crack-up. The chateau was really conducive to work because you couldn't yield to temptation and just drive to London. There were no phone calls because the French telephone system was so bad. You were in the middle of nowhere so you just stayed put for three weeks and did what you had to do."

Elton was desperately tired and avoided a complete crack-up by taking a long-planned and much-needed holiday at Malibu Beach in July. "When I got off the plane," he recalled, "people said to me, 'Hey! You're having a nervous breakdown.' The news had got there that fast. I had glandular fever and was on the verge of a crack-up. I was getting moody and shouting at people, personality-wise I was unbearable. I'd had bouts of exhaustion before but had never been in a nervous state like that."

Fame and Fortune

But whatever the pressures, Elton would never have gone willingly into a long seclusion. Nor is he likely to do so. "Fame can make you into a withdrawn case," he once said. "Look at George Harrison, Dylan, Presley, Lennon and Cassidy. They rarely go out. I love success, if I didn't enjoy it, what would be the point? But I know a lot of stars who don't get enjoyment from it and are really miserable. I love going out, I'm not going to be a hermit for anyone. Mind you, when you get plagued by autograph hunters in the middle of a meal, that's a bit of an aggravation." On another occasion he declared, "Sometimes it's a bit of a drag when you go out — always being recognized. You feel like a monkey in a cage. But if you cut yourself off, you start getting paranoid, you have to try to lead a normal life. Even if you have to sign a hundred autographs when shopping, you have to grin and bear it. You can't tell them to get lost or they might not buy your next record."

One of Elton's first visitors at the rented luxury Malibu mansion in which he was relaxing, was British movie producer Bryan Forbes, who was planning a TV documentary about the star with the working title "Reg." Among his dinner guests during a highly social stay was Groucho Marx. "I was delighted when such a legendary figure accepted my invitation," says Elton. "It was a hot night but I'd been told that as he was old, he would want a log fire burning, so we lit one. For a while before dinner he sat in the lounge talking — wearing his beret and an overcoat. He insisted on calling me John Elton! Most of the time you couldn't tell whether he was serious or poking quiet fun."

Elton Dietrich

Many rock artists have a yen for the history of their own scene but Elton goes much further. "I am very nostalgic — but not just for the '50s," he says. "I'm very much a legend man. I really like legends. That includes those who made their names, retired and became recluses. People like Garbo, Mae West and Groucho are high on my list. So are departed stars like Noel Coward and Laurel and Hardy."

Among legendary stars, Katharine Hepburn has become a special friend and he tells a story about her that is characteristic of the lady. "One day I was sitting at home by the pool waiting for her to come for tea and to have a swim. She came cycling up and I said there was a frog in the pool. 'I'm scared of frogs,' she said. Then she fished the frog out. I asked how she had done it, since she was scared of frogs. She said: 'Character, dear boy, character!'"

There was the time in London when Elton went backstage after watching a Marlene Dietrich show. "I was spellbound by Marlene," he recalls. "She had such presence. She was mesmeric. When I left the stage door, there were people asking for my autograph. I signed one book and then hurried towards my car — still in a daze. The girl to whom I'd given the autograph chased after me. Shoving her book under my nose she exclaimed, 'Look! You've signed Marlene Dietrich!'"

During his Californian holiday Elton met David Cassidy in Hollywood and found that they got on well together. "David is a nice guy," he said. "Some people may knock him but I think he has a lot of talent." Elton asked David to stay at "Hercules"

when he visited Britain in the late summer of 1972. But the request was politely — and thoughtfully — turned down. Cassidy knew only too well that such a visit was likely to result in the house and the surrounding area being besieged by thousands of hysterical fans.

Elton at the time was preparing for another tour of the States and his disc situation there certainly promised well for it. "Honky Chateau" had hit the top of the album charts and another track from it, "Honky Cat," had followed "Rocket Man" into the best-selling singles.

He had just done a British tour sporting a sliver-striped tail coat, red velvet trousers with knee-high green silk cuffs, lurex socks of varying hues and silver platform boots marked E and J in red. His hair was silver, too. "I'm not the best-looking guy around," he said, "so I like to do humorous things. Mick Jagger can wear anything and look good. My clothes are deliberately stupid. I've always looked so ridiculous, people have had to laugh."

That's Entertainment!

Elton's love of the ridiculous spilled over into the staging of his concerts which were beginning to reflect his passion for the glamor and spectacle of the '30s screen musicals. For this tour he found a kindred spirit of lunacy in "Legs" Larry Smith, a famous member of Britain's Bonzo Dog Doo-Dah Band, who had tap-danced during the track "Kill Myself" on "Honky Chateau." Elton and Legs had become close friends sharing a common love of showmanship in the high tradition. Legs was brought into the British tour and then into the American one.

Larry's function was hardly to creep on stage and hide in a corner. His first entrance was made during "Kill Myself" — his rig being immense football shoulder pads, short trousers, tap shoes and a crash helmet mounted with a cardboard wedding couple — when he launched into a dazzling tap sequence. His second appearance was made in a French-style mac and black hat, with umbrella; he handed a twin outfit to Elton, who nipped behind a screen to change and the duo then danced and sang "Singing In The Rain" while being showered with glitter dust. To top this spectacular extravaganza and delight the audience even further, a dozen platinum blondes — as if from a Busby Berkeley movie — tapped their way alongside.

Larry Smith later said of Elton: "What he needed was an outlet for this amazing love of showbiz welling up inside him. It needed to get out

because he's so damned good at it. But just in case the proceedings needed further brightening, Legs Larry appeared later in the tour with a bridal veil flowing from the crash helmet and held at the other end by two midgets; after joining in the tap-dance the midgets then ran off, one returning to hand Mr Smith a bouquet.

What was so impressive was that on top of the razzamatazz, Elton and crew gained profuse critical praise for their music. As one reporter wrote after a super-colossal show before 22,000 at Los Angeles Forum: "Just before midnight Elton and the band finally fell off stage. Soaked with sweat and elated beyond any pitch they had known before, the only reaction they could give was to fall into each others arms and weep."

Jamaica Jamboree

The second chateau-made album had been titled "Don't Shoot Me, I'm Only The Piano Player" and "Crocodile Rock," a track from it, made the British charts late in 1972. Early in 1973, it was followed by another track "Daniel" and "Crocodile Rock" scored in the States as well. Around the same time, the album itself was a hit both sides of the Atlantic, topping the two charts within three weeks of release.

In the meantime came the recording sessions that never were. Elton had wanted the chateau during February but it was to be closed for that month. He then thought Jamaica would be a delightful setting and Gus Dudgeon flew out to check over the studios there He reported that the people running them had said they had, or would get, equipment on a par with that at the chateau, and thus reassured Elton and company headed for the Caribbean.

But he found no time to take advantage of the sun, sea and sand that the island had to offer in abundance. Instead he launched into a spate of creativity. "It was great, the way the writing went in Jamaica," he recalls. "I stuck at it in the studio for the first few days while the rest of the party went around the island. Soon I'd finished 20 songs which was unbelievable! We began rehearsing them and two others left over from our previous sessions at the chateau and we got it so we could have gone on stage right away and performed all 22. But then the piano we wanted didn't arrive, nor some of the mikes. We tried recording with what we had but it didn't sound right so we called a meeting and decided to cut our losses. I was sorry things had gone wrong, if they hadn't, we might have got a good sound there."

The rest of the band made their way back to Britain while Elton opted for an informal flying business trip across the States, taking time off at one stop to have his hair dyed red. Elton's genius for self-publicity and smile-raising eccentricity spread from his on-stage persona into his private and even business life.

Rocket Launch

His extraordinary appearance and love of the bizarre brightened many occasions. For his 26th birthday party, he hired a yacht on the River Thames where he greeted his guests in orange-and-green hair. At the time, he already owned 23 pairs of glasses with another three pairs waiting at Customs. Most of them had been made by a Hollywood firm which specialized in outrageous frames and carried a ready supply of colored lenses. On order was what was to be Elton's optic masterpiece: a pair proclaiming ELTON which flashed on and off.

When he came to launch his own record company, Rocket, his characteristic bravura came to the fore. To a peaceful English country village there came one day in May, 1973, the strangest invasion in its history — a trainload of pop performers, journalists, photographers, TV and radio folk, record company officials, musicians and Elton. From the tiny station they marched — to the bewilderment of the locals — behind a silver band to the ancient, high-beamed village hall where a good time was had by all. The roistering went on for several hours at the hall and continued on the train back to London. At Paddington Station, Elton handed Rocket albums to the departing guests, this time to the bewilderment of commuters.

He brought his promotional flair to bear in the following July when he went to a Beverly Hills party to launch Rocket in the States. He wore blue pumps with white socks, white satin shorts with red piping, a green-and-blue plaid blazer decked with French cigarette labels and, patriotically, heart-shaped glasses with red, white and blue frames.

Super-successful though Elton's previous tours of the States had been, they were eclipsed by his fantastic series of shows which started on August 15, 1973, and ran till October 21. House records set by Elvis and the Stones were broken and at some venues, sold out well ahead, extra shows were added. At Kansas City's Arrowhead Stadium, normally used for football, the audience was estimated to be 28,000, but probably the most spectacular show the star had ever

done — was at the Hollywood Bowl on September 7.

In what resembled a film set from the golden days of Hollywood, actress Linda Lovelace, hostess for the evening, announced the star of the show with a succession of superlatives.

On stage were five grand pianos of different colors. Down the steps came Elton, dressed in a white-and-silver jump suit lavishly decked with ostrich feathers and a matching hat which must have weighed as much as he did. As the piano lids were raised in sweeping unison, they spelt E-L-T-O-N. As they were opened, they released 400 white doves that fluttered over the audience and cheers from the 25,000 fans filled the Bowl. Elton went to the piano and erupted into a barrage of music. He was still in full swing two exhausting hours later.

As one experienced critic wrote: "This was show business in the true sense of the term. All the glamor and glitter that typified Hollywood of old, oozed from Elton John." It was incredible success all along the line for an amazing performer — traveling, as he did, in a private, lavishly luxurious Boeing.

Despite his hectic schedule of concert dates and the inevitable drain on his energy, Elton never showed any signs of flagging vitality in his music. The third chateau-recorded sessions resulted in what was arguably his finest album to date. "Goodbye Yellow Brick Road" was astonishingly successful in both artistic and commercial terms. Released late in '73, it stormed up the charts in both Britain and the States and met with well-deserved critical acclaim.

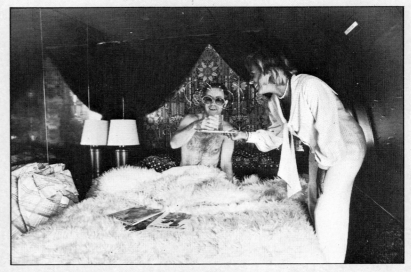

The jet with a difference, where luxury is ludicrous.

Terry O'Neill

In the meantime his business venture, Rocket Records, was lifting off and further satisfaction came for him in the success of Kiki Dee, one of the label's first signings, who had long been admired by critics and people in the business but who had recorded for years without a big hit.

Under the guidance of a record company devoted to fostering talent and with the advantage of a hauntingly beautiful John/Taupin composition called "Amoureuse," the talent she'd shown for so long was finally realized. The song became a British hit and Kiki's career received a valuable additional boost when she and her band played on the same bill as Elton in a series of concerts.

Elton John's status as a major superstar was now confirmed by the screening of Bryan Forbes's documentary. That a filmmaker as well known as Forbes — whose credits as an actor, writer, producer or director, included *The Guns of Navarone, Only Two Can Play, The L-Shaped Room* and *A Shot in the Dark* — should decide to do a documentary on Elton Hercules was an accolade in itself and Forbes's admiration for him was evident.

Musical Mistakes

The film was eventually titled "Elton John and Bernie Taupin Say Goodbye Norma Jean And Other Things" and was screened in Britain on December 4, 1973, being, with reservations, generally well received by the critics. The British version ran 52 minutes but when, early in 1974, it was bought by the ABC network for coast-to-coast screening, they decided that viewers in the States would want to see more, so the American film ran 90 minutes.

Elton topped off a strenuous and hugely successful year with a riproaring series of Christmas shows in London. Indeed, so hectic and exhausting had his schedule been that commentators were observing how cheerfully he had been coping with his relentless work schedule of writing, recording and performing. There were no plans for a let-up at the start of 1974.

For the next album, Elton had chosen studios far from the chateau and traveled with the band to the mountains of Colorado where the Caribou studios were situated on a ranch near Denver. Caribou was the base of Jim Guercio — producer of discs by Chicago, Blood, Sweat and Tears and other top performers. But musically, the ten days of recording there were a disappointment to Elton and colleagues. "Our mistake," Gus Dudgeon said later, "was to turn

Caribou into an English recording studio." Elton and the band had to leave for shows in Japan and the album, called "Caribou," was finished there before going on to tour Australia and New Zealand.

It was mid-March when the group returned to Britain and that was when the grueling programme he had undertaken started to take its toil. So punishing a life must inevitably leave a performer drained and Elton, who had previously taken a physical and mental hammering that brought him to the very brink of breakdown in '72, had been pushing himself far too hard. Fifteen dates set up throughout Britain in April and May had to be canceled, because, as a spokesman for Rocket explained, "Recent tours have left everyone exhausted."

This was something of an understatement. It was only later that the full extent of Elton's exhaustion was revealed, along with the startling news that during this period he had seriously considered quitting the business altogether. For a man who so patently enjoyed his success and reveled in performing, the mere contemplation of retirement must indicate how utterly depressed he was feeling.

The Sporting Life

He was fortunate indeed that during a difficult time in his life, he was surrounded by people who loved and understood him, who would willingly rally round to give him the help and comfort he needed. He paid them tribute after the crisis by declaring: "It was the band, my manager and friends who pulled me through." It says much for Elton's personality that he could inspire such loyalty in those he worked with. He recovered sufficiently to do charity shows in May. One was for Watford — the soccer team he had supported since boyhood. The other — honoring a promise to Princess Margaret several months earlier — was for the Invalid Children's Society. Apart from these, he shunned work and all its pressures.

He relaxed at home, watched soccer, trained with his favorite soccer team, played cricket, watched the Wimbledon tennis championships and even practised with Billie Jean King — now a friend of long standing. Later, he spent a month at a tennis ranch in Arizona. "Tennis," he maintains, "is the only sport at which I am any good." Elton has special esteem for sports stars. "I have more heroes in sport than anywhere else," he says "There's

A superstar with a sportswoman, Elton and Billie Jean King.

ar more dedication in being a tennis champion, for instance, than being a rock musician. I'm sure the Stones don't get up every morning and have a band rehearsal!''

Although Elton may have been having doubts about his own future in rock, his fans, ignorant of these uncertainties, were progressing his career regardless. Despite the band's reservations, ''Caribou'' was a monster hit in the summer of 1974 and so was a single ''Don't Let The Sun Go Down On Me,'' which had been taken from it. Moreover, Elton had signed a new American contract with MCA Records, said to be worth a colossal $8,000,000 and making him the highest paid artist in disc history. Refreshed by his lay-off, he returned to Caribou for some summer sessions that were approached very differently from the first ones. He and the band crossed the Atlantic on the SS France in June and rehearsed on board.

While in New York, Elton went to see John Lennon with whom he had become friendly in Los Angeles the previous year and was invited to join the sessions for two tracks on his ''Walls and Bridges'' album. When Elton learned that Lennon was going to Los Angeles to work on a song he'd written for Ringo, he said, ''Why not come to Caribou on the way back? We'll be doing 'Lucy In The Sky.' '' Lennon accepted.

The second Caribou album was provisionally to be called ''Captain Fantastic And The Brown Dirt Cowboy.'' Material for it had been written aboard the SS France and it was basically about the John/Taupin experiences from their first meeting up to the ''Empty Sky'' album. Lennon's help on the new album included singing with Elton on ''Lucy'' — later a vast hit. A rapport developed between the two musicians: ''John works the way I do in the studio,'' said Elton. ''We just had a laugh and I really have a very strong affection for him.''

Wizard in Boots

After such comprehensive success, the next obvious step for Elton was the movies. He had done a small guest spot in Marc Bolan's *Born to Boogie*, but his personality, seemingly so suited to an extrovert film cameo, hadn't been utilized until controversial director Ken Russell sought his services for the film version of The Who's rock opera, *Tommy*. Elton took the part of the Pinball Wizard and managed to look entirely at home in what must

ate as the world's largest pair of boots. They were extraordinary and gigantic examples of footwear that nearly doubled his height. Performing his scenes in them demanded a generous allowance of guts and daring.

When he had completed the shooting, Elton left in October for a 44-city tour of the States and Canada with Kiki Dee and her band. Again, his tour was to be by the Boeing billed as "the largest, most luxurious and most expensive jetliner in the world." The tour was an astounding success, even by John standards and it is estimated his shows were watched by 750,000 with a total box office of $5,000,000. As usual top stars flocked to see him. When he returned to Los Angeles for a four-night stand at the 18,700-seat Inglewood Forum, the out-fronters included Liz Taylor, Barbra Streisand, David Cassidy, Diana Ross, Ringo Starr and Harry Nilsson.

John and John

At New York's Madison Square Garden near the end of the tour, John Lennon came on stage to join in three numbers. "Originally," says Elton, "I told John, 'Let's do two numbers. Then you'll have to do a third.' I suggested 'Imagine.' He replied, 'Oh no! Boring. I've done it before. Let's do a rock & roll song.' So I thought of 'I Saw Her Standing There' — first track on the first Beatles' album. And it hadn't been John singing it, but McCartney. John was so knocked out at my suggestion, because he'd not sung the lead before."

On came Lennon to join with Elton on the former Beatle's latest hit, "Whatever Gets You Thru' The Night" and then the spotlight focused on Elton as he went into "Lucy In The Sky" with Lennon joining him on the chorus. Then, in his familiar nasal voice, Lennon told the crowd, "We were trying to think of a number to get me offstage so I can be sick. We came up with this one — written by my fiancé Paul." So Lennon sang "Standing There" with a little help from his friend and left the stage accompanied by hysterical acclaim. The number was such a success that Elton even repeated it in London without Lennon's help.

"For us it was very emotional," said Elton later. "Nobody could believe it. I knew John would be petrified but he really enjoyed it. I was more scared than he was — hoping things would go right for him. I wish he could have

Top: Elton, Bolan and Ringo at the premiere of "Born to Boogie."
Right: Lennon's guest appearance.

done more numbers because the reaction was so great, but he wanted to go upstairs and be sick. He told me he used to throw up before he went on stage. He came to Boston to see us before we did New York and I've never seen anyone so nervous in my life. He was so worried for us. Then it affected me at Madison Square, when he was quite calm and just wanted to get it over. Obviously he got a big kick out of the reaction for him. It was incredible!''

Elton also reported a compliment from the former Beatle: "John says he doesn't know how we do it, the Beatles' act used to be 20 minutes and he says he used to think that was an hour. An eternity for him. He said, 'There were four of us and you do two and a half hours. How the hell do you do it?' I explained that most people do that now. He will always say the pressure wasn't as great on him as it is on me or someone else, but I wouldn't have been in his shoes. I just couldn't have taken it.''

So sensational were the concerts that one seasoned critic, just after the tour, was prompted to say that Elton was "approaching the status of being acclaimed as the world's top entertainer.''

Supreme Showman

Entertainment, a dedication to giving the public great value for their money and a huge appetite for enjoying his work are at the root of Elton John's philosophy as a performer. Through hard work and dazzling professionalism, he earns every plaudit that is heaped upon him. After his 1974 Christmas shows in London, which had the audience howling for more, a critic particularly praised "a man and his musicians packing more solid entertainment into one show than most artists put into half a year's work.'' Another was inspired to say, "His sheer professionalism is a lesson to pop artists who think anything will do for the fans.''

Add to this phenomenal showmanship his brilliant musical ability plus an unusually close working relationship with an extremely talented lyricist, and the secret of Elton John's success is revealed. As an artist and a man, his most striking characteristic is his boundless enthusiasm; he throws himself so completely into his work, his life and his pursuit of fun, and gives so much of himself in his performances, both on stage and disc, that no one can begrudge him his fame, his popularity or his wealth.

By late '74, "Elton John's Greatest Hits'' was topping the album charts in the States and Britain — with MCA saying that it was the fastest-selling disc in their history. "Lucy In The Sky'' was yet another huge hit, although Elton received some criticism for recording Beatle material. He answered the charge with the simple claim that a great song would always stand the test of time.

Also of great satisfaction to Elton during the closing weeks of 1974 were the appearances in the American singles charts of Kiki Dee's "I Got The Music In Me'' (Rocket's first Stateside hit) and Neil Sedaka's "Laughter In The Rain.'' Neil has laughingly dubbed Elton: "The most expensive publicist in the world.'' Certainly, he has played a vital part in Neil's resurgence in the States — following the one which had already happened in Britain.

Widest Range

The two met at a Sedaka party in London early in 1973 and, when Elton realized that Neil had no current American label, he was quick to suggest that he sign with Rocket for the States, a proposition which Neil readily accepted. Later Elton was a visitor at Neil's London apartment where they discussed plans for Neil's new disc career in the States. "I had been a Sedaka fan, anyway,'' says Elton. "So the basic plan was as simple as finding out what he wanted to have on his album — which turned out to be a compilation from his British albums. It had been like Elvis coming up and giving us the chance to release his records. We couldn't believe our luck.''

Later, when Neil's "Bad Blood'' single was released in Britain with Elton playing on it, the latter commented, "I only appear on the records of people I really know or like.'' Both Elton and Neil have stressed the similarities between them. Each had classical piano training when young, each is a singer/composer, each appeals to a wide span of age groups and to tastes ranging from underground to middle-of-the-road and each has a vast zeal for performing.

With "Captain Fantastic'' set for release in the spring, Elton flew to Los Angeles early in 1975 for a TV show which would probably earn him in four days what some men earn in 50 years. But who was to say he didn't deserve it, or when it would end? Elton has no idea. With his usual endearing modesty and candidly self-mocking humor he dodges the issue and jokes that aged 60: "I'll be a bald pub pianist playing 'Your Song' with people shouting for the latest Top 20 hits. As long as his gift is his song, it's unlikely to come to that.

RECREATIONS

Not every artist within the rock-music world has his personal life described in such detail as Elton John. Yet Reginald Kenneth Dwight, with all his personal likes and dislikes, is described in great detail, in the musical press from teen magazines to *Rolling Stone*.

Rolling Stone is hardly worried by the kind of factual data once provided for its readers by Britain's highest teen-selling paper, *Jackie*. *Jackie* told of Elton's cocker spaniel called Brian and German Shepherd, Bruce. *Rolling Stone* once gave space to a description of the property Elton rented whilst he was staying in one of his favorite places, Los Angeles.

Apart from mentioning the presence of 500 Qualatex balloons with the insignia of the current tour imprinted upon their skins, picture books on Maxfield Parrish, Dali and Disney, a

S.K.R.

London Features International

TV and videocassette unit, the writer also briefly described the sight of record albums stacked neatly against a bookshelf.

It is, indeed, an abiding passion of Elton's to hear and assess all recorded music. When off-duty from recording, rehearsing, and the basics required of a star from the media industry, Elton makes his way toward the large record stores and spends liberally. Friends say

Far left: Dressed for cricket. Left: Clowning on the soccer pitch with superstars Rod Stewart and Michael Parkinson. Below: Sporting the Union Jack.

I'M BACK IN
GREAT BRITAIN
AND WATFORD

S.I.

he buys literally everything which is new since his last visit. Not surprisingly the same people speak in some wonder at the vastness of his personal record library, a collection enhanced a year or so back when he bought a collection of '50s records which ran into thousands.

Elton's love for music other than his own leads him into forays on radio stations, particularly American ones, where he willingly spins his disc selection for hours.

But music is only one major recreational activity. British record-paper readers know Elton best for his undoubted love and passion for the British major supported game of soccer.

Elton is a Vice-President of Watford Football Club, the nearest major British league football team to his home area of Pinner, though in footballing terms the club would have difficulty in staking any claim to being in Britain's top 50 teams.

Apart from flying home from America to watch their progress, and making constant Atlantic calls to ascertain their current fortune during the season, Elton also gives the Club considerable financial aid. On one occasion he organized a major pop concert and netted a substantial sum of money for the Club.

American fans hear more about his tennis exploits, particularly his strong friendship with Wimbledon triple winner, Billie Jean King. Yet Elton's tennis interest extends back to his younger days, though in those days he could not, as now, command coaching and help from Ken Rosewall and Arthur Ashe.

As a player, his standard is described as "good" but tennis, like his discjockeying, needs personal commitment of an active kind, whereas other Elton recreational pursuits rely on appreciating the skill and work of others. He avidly collects works of art and various kinds of antiques. He revels in the humor of Monty Python, Tommy Cooper, and Stanley Baxter and is a fervent fan of the British television series, *Coronation Street*.

Apart from picture books Elton keeps numerous biographies. For example, while his hired British Airways 707 winged the waters with its guests, Elton was reading the biography of the Duchess of Windsor.

When his committments will allow Elton likes to follow the pattern which suits him best. He takes ten hours of sleep/recreation and unlike many pop stars who only rise at midday, he meets the world and his records at 8 a.m.

Elton relaxing in the luxury of his drawing room at home, surrounded by books, works of art and antiques.

44

Ian Vaughan/Transworld

BERNIE AND ELTON

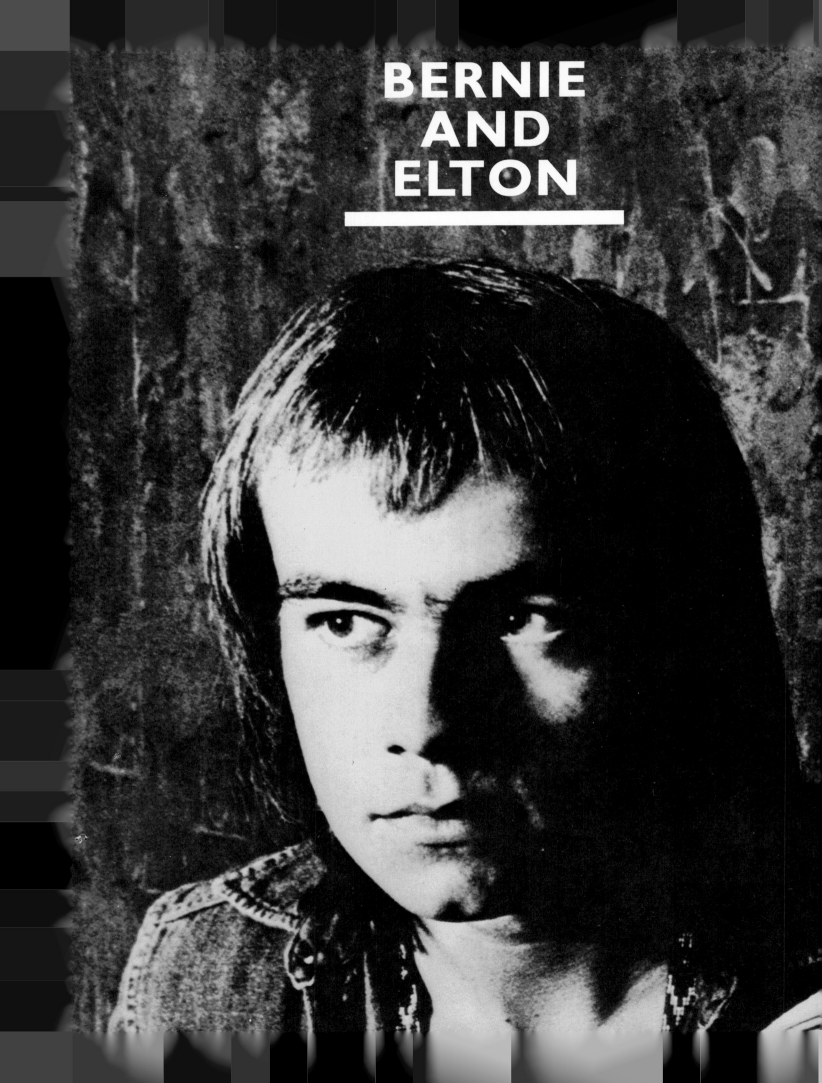

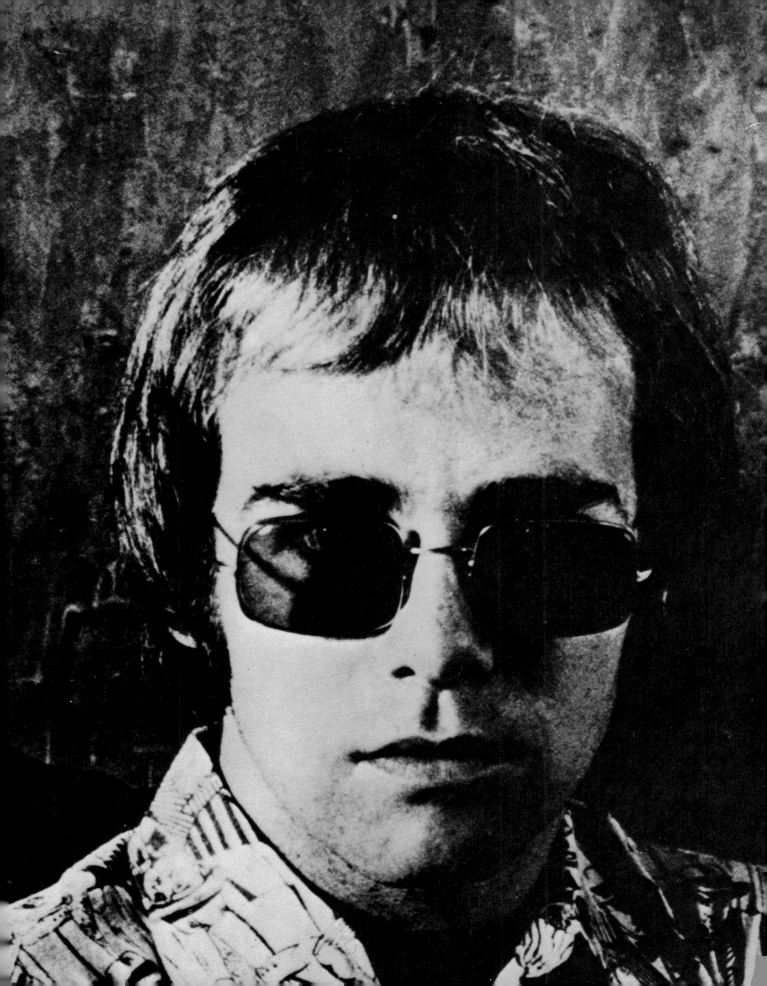

Summed up in print, it seems so simple. Bernie Taupin writes the words. He hands them to Elton. Or even posts them to him. Elton sticks the word sheet on the piano. Half-an-hour later he has the music.

If you can write music for a song which will appeal to millions in 30 minutes, there is only one word to describe it: genius. But that is not to deny the talent of the man who wrote the words in the first place.

Bernie Taupin was born on May 22, 1950, in Lincolnshire, England. His father worked for Britain's Ministry of Agriculture and Bernie was raised in a rural atmosphere which gave him a preference for the country over the city that has never left him.

Bernie, who had been "a bookworm since childhood" started writing poetry at school and, after leaving, gravitated towards journalism, working in a technical capacity on a local newspaper — "The Lincolnshire Chronicle."

He'd maintained his interest in the written word and, with hopes of a career as a lyricist, he first met Elton late in 1967 at Dick James House in London. He was waiting in the reception area when Reg Dwight came from an inner office to ask, "Is there a lyricist here?" They went out for a coffee and that was when it all began to happen.

Long Range Writing

"I only started to write songs when I met Reg," said Bernie a long time later. "The first bundle of words I handed him were poetry. They hadn't been written with music in mind." During the early months of their partnership, they saw little of each other. Bernie would write words in Lincolnshire and when he had a stack of them he would come to London, take them from his briefcase and hand them to Elton who would then go away and write the music. They would meet again to check on the finished songs and there was rarely any disagreement about the treatment.

"People find it hard to believe the way we work," said Elton late in 1968. "But that's the way it is. I don't interfere with Bernie's words because I couldn't write them, and he wouldn't dream of writing a melody. It works, though, because we both dig what the other is doing."

After a period of getting to know each other and finding that they were on the same wavelength, there came

a spell when they were in close contact. "The country boy came to London," Bernie recalls. "Elton and I took a flat. It was freezing cold and we practically starved, but we were lucky enough to find people who encouraged us to write what we felt instead of just trying to be commercial. Then Elton and the band went to America in 1970 and things became better and better."

Fame might have come to Elton, but from the very start he insisted that Bernie's indispensable part in the partnership be fully stressed at all times. Just after that breakthrough tour of the States he declared: "If it wasn't for Bernie, there wouldn't be any songs. It's very easy for me to do my part, to write a song to Bernie's lyrics is the most natural thing for me to do.

"I've never given Bernie melodies to put lyrics to because I never get ideas for melodies till after he's done the words." Then he added the illuminating statement: "Bernie's words draw melodies out of me."

Inner Meanings?

What of Bernie's own inspiration? He once confessed of his initial efforts at lyric writing: "The first stuff I wrote was dreadful. I mean really disgusting, pre-'Sgt. Pepper' things about 'freaked-out teddy bears.' I'd never experienced anything, I was just a hick who thought that if I wanted to make the big time I had to have freak-out lyrics. I was really young and stupid." But once he and Elton had started to make their mark on the disc scene, it was clear that "dreadful" was the last adjective to be applied to Bernie's lyrics.

Though he wrote love songs, a major inspiration in those days was nostalgia, "the way things used to be." The atmosphere of America's southern states, old movies, early rock — all were subject matter for his lyrics. But his efforts were not free from misrepresentation. At one point, after remarking that his recent lyrics included some which were straightforward modern pieces and a couple which were plain banal, he was prompted to add: "At least people won't be able to read into these all the amazing things they used to with some of the early songs. Nobody in America seemed to take them at face value. They came up with incredible things like racialism, anti-Semitism in 'Border Song' — and someone said 'I Need You To Turn To' was about the Crucifixion!"

Agreeing that, taken on its own, "Burn Down The Mission" was a very strong revolutionary song, he declared, "But it's meant to be about the Ameri-

can Civil War and I think it cools it a bit if you see Elton singing it, because he doesn't look that serious. It's kind of silly that "Mission" has become a rallying song for revolutionaries in the States."

In his youth Bernie had been an ardent follower of early rock and he later described some of the lyrics of that era as "marvelously evocative." He went on: "All the best people of the time were the ones whose lyrics related to the life kids were leading. I mean, for example, the Beach Boys. Some of Brian Wilson's early surfing lyrics were ridiculously good. Also Eddie Cochran, he would have been a writing force today had he lived."

Consistently, the rapport between lyricist and composer has been phenomenal. "When I get Bernie's lyrics," Elton once said, "I know exactly what he is talking about." At the same time — giving a fascinating insight into their working relationship — Bernie declared that when he wrote a lyric, he always had a preconceived melody in his head. "Amazingly," he added, "Elton's melodies are always exactly as I had hoped." And the duo have consistently shown they can maintain this rapport even when geographically apart, so that they have understandably described their joint creativity as "telepathic."

Spontaneous Songs

The flatmates broke up when Bernie went to live in Lincolnshire again after marrying an American girl, Maxine, to whom he had dedicated 'Tiny Dancer,' on "Madman Across The Water." Elton and Bernie continued to go their own way over the years, creating their music spontaneously and never consciously tailoring their efforts for sure-fire chart success. Indeed Elton has declared that he has no idea if a song is likely to be a hit. He cited as an example of this "Bennie And The Jets" — a track from the "Goodbye Yellow Brick Road" album. This was not a studio recording but a tape of a show Elton had done at London's Royal Festival Hall and two years later Gus Dudgeon recommended its addition to the album. "I would never have released 'Bennie And The Jets' as a single in America," declared Elton. "But it has been our biggest selling single so far."

Elton has said that "the kids want noise, not melody." And added, "Years ago they liked trad jazz because it made them want to dance, as did rock when that came in. Critics said rock & roll would die, but fifteen years later it still hasn't died and I don't think it ever will. The kids will always

want their eardrums splattered." There may be a lot of truth in that but this is not to deny for a moment the high general quality of John/Taupin songs and the fact that people listening to them, both live and on disc, are constantly impressed by their durability.

Norma Jean

Elton, on the other hand, has likened their songs to bottles of milk or postage stamps — used and soon forgotten — and added that he has great difficulty in remembering his own songs after, say, a couple of years. Modestly, he says he hopes that perhaps two or three will become standards — possibly "Your Song," "Daniel" and "Candle In The Wind."

The last — a hauntingly beautiful tribute to Marilyn Monroe — is described by Elton as: "The only song Bernie and I have ever written which gives me goose bumps every time I play it." Bernie has said of the song, "The more I read about Marilyn, the more I was fascinated. 'Candle In The Wind' was the phrase which came to me to picture her life. Once I had that title, it spurred me to write the lyrics."

Late in 1973, after a lot of searching, Bernie and Maxine found just the home they wanted — a Georgian mansion with a large garden just down the road from Elton with room to house the hundreds of books he had collected over the years. In addition to his songwriting, he is a prolific writer of children's poetry and has written a book about his work with Elton — including details of how some of his lyrics came to be written — called, with wry humor, "The One Who Writes The Words."

Although preferring to keep in the background, Bernie has been on stage with Elton and the band. The first time was at Madison Square Garden in September, 1973. "I was just standing in the wings minding my own business," he recalls, "when the band came off. They were called back for an encore and as they went on, Elton and Davey Johnstone dragged me with them. As I stood on stage, absolutely petrified, someone shoved a tambourine into my hand and I rattled it about during two encores. Looking back, I suppose it was quite funny, but at the time, I was so nervous I almost turned and ran."

Bernie Taupin is not one for the limelight, though. He has expressed his own personality in very simple terms: "I'm really just a romantic at heart. But then I think everybody is." And that, perhaps, is the fundamental secret of his success.

ELTON AND BLUESOLOGY

Around 1964 a new semi-professional group emerged in the Harrow area of Middlesex, a location some 15 or so miles from central London.

Elton, pianist at the Northwood Hills Hotel on Thursdays, Fridays, and Saturdays, joined this group and later with the other band members became professional, once they had successfully auditioned for the Roy Tempest agency and started their role of backing visiting US soul acts.

The first Bluesology, of which Elton was part, comprised Stuart Brown, guitar and vocal; Mick Inkpen, drums; Rex Bishop, bass; and of course Elton himself, on organ.

They played local halls and with their lead singer, Stuart Brown, a devoted Jimmy Witherspoon fan, played numbers like "Times Are Getting Tougher Than Tough"; their choice of material was not always popular with the audiences who merely wanted loud noise. Elton's head was absorbed in the rock & roll heroes whose music at the time was busily being released on the famed London American label and played on Radio Luxembourg by Tony Hall.

The Tempest Agency contract led Bluesology into the world of Patti LaBelle & Her Bluebells, one of whose members, Cindy Birdsong, later found fame with the Supremes. They backed Major Lance and would have done the same for Wilson Pickett, only the singer found them wanting, musically.

Bluesology left the Tempest Agency and joined Marquee Artists and found themselves on the posh trendy club circuit, as well as playing less aristocratic places as the famed Liverpool Cavern and the Top Ten in Hamburg. They played about 10 gigs a week, doubling at weekends with each member receiving around £15 a week. They had no radios.

For Elton, such a world as this at first proved exciting. Apart from backing many well-known names from America, although he found many of these disappointing, the club circuit and particularly the London scene led to his hearing and seeing then revered idols like Mike Bloomfield, The Beatles, and Gene Pitney.

Periodically Elton went through a close self-examination with regard to his future. He had ambitions of being a vocalist, and indeed had sung on Bluesology's first ever released single, "Come Back Baby". He tired of endless nights playing standard soul numbers and yet found himself in a quandary, for as he told John Tobler in Britain's monthly, *Zig Zag*, "I had to do something and I didn't want to join another band because quite honestly, I wasn't that good an organist and I didn't look that good either. Really, I wanted to be a singer – but who would consider employing me in that capacity?"

From this point the story, except Bluesology's spell with Long John Baldry, basically moves into what is covered elsewhere in this volume, namely Elton's work at Mills Music, his meeting with Bernie Taupin and work at DJM. But one aspect of early Elton remains: his involvement with session and demo recording.

One demo was very personal for it comprised around 10 tracks of his own writing, recorded on a two-track machine! Elton says the tapes are now lost but at the time he thought that they were rather amazing.

He sang and played on music writers' demonstrations of their songs and even, according to Elton, sang backing vocals on the Tom Jones disc, "Daughter Of Darkness", and was the pianist on the massive Hollies smash, "He Ain't Heavy, He's My Brother".

There were endless recordings for budget-price albums, the kind where the current Top 20 are sung by non-credited artists, whose vocal ability

(with musical backing) is said to resemble the "original". One of these recordings was the Stevie Wonder composition, "Signed, Sealed, Delivered I'm Yours", a recording with which Elton seems particularly pleased.

Several of the early Elton-Bernie Taupin songs were recorded. One called "The Tide Will Turn For Rebecca" was put on disc by Edward Woodward, and there was a degree of success with "I Can't Go On Living Without You" which was entered for selection, along with hundreds of others, for Britain's entry in the Eurovision Song Contest. It reached the top six and was later recorded by Liverpool's Cilla Black.

At this point Reg Dwight became Elton John and "I've Been Lovin' You" was released and promptly died a quick death. A particularly depressing period followed for Bernie and Elton. The answer to their musical problems came in some simple but perceptive advice from DJM plugger, Steve Brown. He told the two they would do better if they wrote what they wanted and were not forever tailoring material to suit others.

This led to the duo writing songs which appeared on "Empty Sky" and "Lady Samantha". Soon they were well away on the road which leads to fame and riches.

Early pictures of Elton John – released by Dick James Music at the time of Bluesology.

Behind the glitter, beneath the fun, below the showbiz trappings there lies another Elton John — the consummate musician. The phenomenon that is Elton John simply couldn't survive at the pitch and pace that it has on pure showmanship. It is founded on a bedrock of creative ability and sheer talent that have produced some of the best and most popular songs since the Beatles.

The John/Taupin partnership has spawned music that is not only memorable and catchy enough for the charts, but also has a breadth of subject matter and a depth of intensity and feeling to ensure that it will last long after the ephemeral fads of rock music have been forgotten.

From their prolific pens have come future standards like "Your Song" and "Daniel," songs that bring a new look to life like "Goodbye Yellow Brick Road" and searingly sensitive revelations like the poignant "Candle In The Wind." In addition, old rock forms have been given a brand new twist in numbers like "Crocodile Rock" and "Saturday Night's Alright For Fighting."

To achieve such a range and to cover so much ground in so short a time as the release of "Empty Sky" in 1969 and the extraordinary "Goodbye Yellow Brick Road" in '74 shows a mature and intelligent approach to music. It's startling how well Elton John and Bernie Taupin mesh together, producing words perfectly attuned to music, to create a piece of work. Perhaps their greatest attribute is their total lack of pretension. Bernie's words are often serious but never self-consciously clever; Elton's music marries to them perfectly because he never considers himself to be a better composer than he really is. If anything, he tends to undervalue his own abilities.

Perhaps the team's most notable achievement has been to reconcile within their music the two main modern music streams of rock and pop. If rock became too over-blown in aspiration and intent in the early '70s and pop was looked down upon as inferior, Elton never took any notice. His music had the sensitivity and experiment of good rock and brought to it the catchiness, appeal and razzamatazz of pop. He welded the two together and made the result entirely his own. He also managed to avoid the easy trap of falling between the two stools and producing a mongrel that would appeal neither to one audience or the other and flop on its face.

The evolution of Elton's music has been fairly rapid. He found a course that suited him after a certain amount of early hesitation and he followed it well without being irked by too many obvious commercial constraints. His early period — the "Empty Sky," "Elton John," "Tumbleweed Connection" and "Madman Across The Water" albums — saw the seed and the roots of most of his work to follow.

The "Elton John" album was stylistically central to the music of the first four studio-produced albums, from "Empty Sky" through to "Madman Across The Water." The mood was generally serious, either low key sentimentality or a semi-gospel howl. The music was dominated by Elton's piano and Paul Buckmaster's string arrangements, the latter becoming increasingly ominous from album to album as Taupin's lyrical concerns darkened towards the depths of "Madman Across The Water."

Romance and Nostalgia

The fact that Elton writes music to Bernie's words, rather than vice versa, obviously gives the words — and Bernie Taupin — a great importance. On the early albums the words tended toward the obscurely romantic but with a breadth of subject-matter that is rare. But it was one of their most obvious compositions, "Your Song," which established them as writers of ingenuous songs. The words here are perfectly complemented by the tender voice and the swaying melody.

The next album, "Tumbleweed Connection," gave full play to Bernie's obsession with Americana, which can be seen in a wider context as an obsession with loss — a deep and yearning nostalgia. This reached its height with "Indian Sunset," on "Madman," which starts with Elton singing unaccompanied, and then introduces a menacingly insistent piano which gradually fades into a nostalgic resignation as the strings take up the theme of barely controlled rage. Strings also dominated the title cut, with its brilliantly evocative opening lines — "I can see very well, there's a boat on the reef with a broken back" — and Elton's singing at its most seriously expressive. "Madman Across The Water," which was the furthest logical extension of the music started on "Empty Sky" and "Elton John," was also the furthest away from "pop" that Elton John was to venture. It also marked the relative nadir of his commercial fortunes. And that point was not to be missed.

The change which came over Elton's music on "Honky Cat" and the following albums, was really no more than a

J. Stevens

change of emphasis. He has always been something of a rock & roller at heart, as a couple of cuts from each of the earlier albums bear witness. Talking once about playing on the Hollies' "He Ain't Heavy," he said that "they thought they were making art. I was just having a good time." The "live" album, "17.11.70," which was released before "Madman," conveyed Elton the raver far more than did any of the studio albums. But his audience, weaned on the singer/songwriter values of the early '70s, didn't want to know. Taupin's lyrics may never have exactly bared his soul, but they did sound serious, and rock & roll was not considered a serious medium. But then again, seriousness was one thing, morbidity was another. Couldn't Elton write "Your Song" over and over again with nice piano and strings? The answer was no — Elton may think his work has built-in obsolescence, but he's serious about the fun he produces. The way out of the impasse had to be a return to more of a pop style but without losing any of the old trademarks.

Chateau Bottled

In early '72, Elton went to France to record in the "Strawberry Studios" Chateau. And this time he had a band with him, not a collection of session men. Folk-guitarist Davey Johnstone, late of Magna Carta, had been added to Dee and Olsson. This, as Elton put it, "took the pressure off the rest of us." Guitar, which until this time had been pretty inconspicuous on Elton's records, now became an important part of the group's sound. The massive string arrangements of the earlier records were cut back accordingly. The result was a clearer sound, in which Elton's voice and piano could be counterpointed by guitar rather than drowned in strings. It was a rock & roll band on record.

This album, produced in France, was suitably called "Honky Chateau." One of the singles taken from it, "Rocket Man," obligingly rocketed up the charts. One of Bernie's most perspective lyrics — the exploration of the cosmos reduced to a lonely job, "burning out my fuse up here alone" — was backed by a flowing melody, interspersed with the electronic wails of a synthesizer. It marked the beginning of Elton's second wave of popularity in Britain, and carried him over the hump in the States, after the over-production in quantity/quality of 1971.

The creative cycle: the hand that makes the music holds the disc.

53

As "Honky Chateau" was becoming Elton's first no. 1 album in the States, the band was already back in France cutting another one, to be titled "Don't Shoot Me, I'm Only The Piano Player." The first side turned out to be "my discotheque album." Three singles were released from the album, two of them in particular — "Daniel" and "Crocodile Rock" — really hitting the jackpot. It is a happy album, a long way from the doom of "Madman." The piano rocks along over Olsson and Dee's thumping beat and Davey plugs in the gaps with some amazing guitar playing for someone who'd only just turned electric. Elton sings like he's really enjoying himself.

The lyrical content had also shifted since "Madman." Bernie's obsession with old America was not so all-pervasive, the '50's music scene and the '40s film scene were rapidly becoming the prime targets for his nostalgia: "long nights crying by the record machine, dreamin' of my Chevy and my old blue jeans." And still on each album there were a couple of gems in the sensitive love song department and numbers on many subjects, from crime to rednecks, from schooldays to teenage idols. In the meantime, Elton swept across the States and Britain playing to packed houses, and becoming more outrageous each time.

Consummate Unity

The "Goodbye Yellow Brick Road" album, released in autumn '73, seemed in many ways to sum up all that had gone before. Being a double album it had space to include just about everything. All the things that Bernie and his audience had lost — the American West, Marilyn Monroe, a simple male chauvinist view of women, '50s rock & roll, sanity — are paraded in an apocalyptic procession. The band really knew each other by this time, and the combination of their musical skills, Elton's singing, and the duo's writing, produced a few really remarkable songs. "Candle In The Wind" about Marilyn, for example, is only flawed by a couple of Taupin's lines (he does have a tendency towards uneven writing within songs). The chorus is perfectly constructed, sung beautifully over a fine, distinctive melody, illuminated by flashes of Davey Johnstone's guitar.

The fine moments on this record suggest that Elton had finally begun to put the pieces of himself together. He seemed to have bridged the gap between pop and rock, between fun and dedication, between being a clown and being an artist. He had always been all of these, but previously the various parts tended to clash slightly. Part of his audience would tug him one way and part the other. Perhaps now he was getting to the point where he could tug them together.

"Saturday Night's Alright For Fighting" is a good example. Perhaps one of the best singles of 1973, Davey's crazy, guitar riff and Elton's rockabilly piano put it in a class of its own. The sheer musical exuberance is staggering. Elton seems to have the ability to synthesize all the various influences on him and create something fresh out of them. He understands the enormous impact that can be achieved by musical simplicity and the clever turning of an old form into contemporary idiom.

The next album, "Caribou" was recorded in the States and was recognizably different from the three French ones. Elton and the group were disappointed with the sessions, feeling that they had attacked the atmosphere of an American recording studio, rather than working with it. It produced one great love song, later released as a single, "Don't Let The Sun Go Down On Me," a fine piece of American nostalgia in "Dixie Lily" and a rocker, "The Bitch Is Back." There was also an interesting piece of British nostalgia in the shape of "Grimsby." Although lacking the consolidated unity of "Goodbye Yellow Brick Road," the album might have marked the beginning of a new phase in Elton's musical development.

A Place in History

Elton's contribution to rock music has been important. If he never recorded another song he would still go down in rock history as being the man who brought refreshing candor and enormous enjoyment to the music. Seldom have so many good songs appeared with such consistency, been recorded with such care and performed with such vigor. The John/Taupin partnership has an almost telepathic closeness when one considers that the two parts are done, not in unison with both composer and lyricist gathered round the piano to fit the words and music together as they go along, but at a distance of many miles.

Elton John has achieved that rare thing in rock — the fusion of good, sometimes great music, with rip-roaring entertainment and he has helped rock save itself from its own overambitiousness. Not a bad boast from someone who swears he's only in it for the fun.

Elton relaxes at home with an almost indecent quantity of Gold Discs proving his musical success.

GOINGS-ON

Although in his pre-teen years Elton John was shy and withdrawn, petrified of communication and a sayer of few words, later times produce colorful stories depicting a more extrovert character.

Even by the age of 12 he was up to tricks. Most Saturdays he did attend his classical class at the Royal Academy of Music, but there were times when he just rode the underground train system. He was always careful to ensure he arrived home at more or less the same time and no one guessed that he had not got off the subway!

He remembers occasions at his local pub, the Northwood Hills Hotel, when tempers flared and the patrons involved themselves in fist fighting. Elton left his usually out-of-tune piano and hurled himself through the windows. Well, it was the only way to escape.

A few years later he recalls mad scenes from Bluesology's frequent gig location at South Harrow British Legion Hall. The group were musically rather snobbish and they played blues à la Jimmy Witherspoon, music with a then very limited "in" following. He can remember rockers riding their bikes into the hall and threatening to smash the group's gear unless they stopped their blues playing and gave the rocker patrons sounds of basic rock & roll.

Journalists recall a much later event during the pre-Christmas period of 1973. Elton was holding court at London's Inn On The Park for the purpose of promoting his Christmas single, "Step Into Christmas", the disc he has always felt bears the "feel" of the Phil Spector-produced Ronettes. At the same time his active mind had contrived a slightly disconcerting event for unsuspecting journalists, individuals well used to long and often boring tirades from superstars.

There was a fold-away bed concealed in the hotel room wall. Elton thought it would be a good idea if he pulled the bed down, lay on it and was folded away into the wall. Then once journalists had had time to sit down and begin to wonder whether the star was intending to show up after all, he could make a sudden and noisy appearance. In the end Elton decided against this prank as he realized it would not be very comfortable being more or less trussed up, and also rather dangerous, being faced with the distinct possibility that the mechanism would not function, thus leaving him in a rather nasty predicament!

Even his mother has been involved in stories with the slightly odd and horrific twist. For many years Elton

S.I.

Terry O'Neill

collected stuffed animals. With both his British and American homes becoming increasingly full it was decided the animals should be given to children's hospitals. This mission was accomplished by Elton's mother, who loaded her car with them and took them round to various hospitals. Unfortunately members of the public didn't realize that the animals were only stuffed and there were reports of frightened individuals removing themselves quickly from the scene when the car parked to unload, or rushing to the telephone to call the police for assistance.

The more serious musical side of Elton has its own stories. When Elton first joined DJM it was in part due to his using DJM studios in the making of trial discs. He did quite a few without being noticed by the hierarchy and was ushered secretly into the studios during lunchtime. Eventually the boss, Dick James, found out and was heard asking in a loud voice, "Who the hell are Reg Dwight and Bernie Taupin?" Fortunately, he heard the trial tapes

and, even if then slightly unimpressed, was astute enough to sign them up.

Elton inspires other people into perhaps simple but nevertheless effective action. During his 1973 Madison Square Garden concert in New York the audience devised a method of getting him to give an encore. They stood in groups and, the idea obviously spreading from one group to the next, lit matches until thousands of these matches burned, creating a spectacle which a specialist showman like Elton could not help but admire, and consequently he gave in to their demands for further music.

Not all Elton happenings have a pleasant twist. For example, there was considerable hassle when the Band was recording in Kingston, Jamaica. A strike had occurred at the Dynamic Sound studio, and with the group mistaken as strike-breakers their Volkswagen bus was sprayed with something akin to crushed fiberglass which came through the window and caused skin rashes.

No pop star or group has yet

Elton's extensive collection of stuffed animals is legendary.

rivaled Elton's amazing "flying and partying" circus of 1975 when he flew more than 100 people to Los Angeles in a hired British Airways 707 jet. The party contained some journalists but basically comprised Elton's family, the staff of his British record company, people from Watford Football Club, and the famous soccer player, Rodney Marsh.

The idea had come from his manager John Reid's birthday party attended by a vast throng and Elton decided that such a lavish event should be repeated. Since he had an important concert at the Dodger Stadium in Los Angeles it seemed a pleasant idea to transport his guests across the Atlantic waters. They could see his concert, view the sights, and go partying.

For Elton this was merely another in a long line of happenings — but what other star has assembled such a motley crowd of people and spent a reported $250,000 just for an event?

59

Elton may not see much good in the general output of American television companies but he has an obvious love for Americans and America. And perhaps one should add the word Americana to this.

Such a love is witnessed even in the early albums before Elton found himself fêted by East Coast audiences and later the darling of the West Coast, and particularly the Los Angeles music-lovers.

"Tumbleweed" and "Elton John" smell of Americana and America in this context is the birthplace of rock & roll and its heroes. Elton and Bernie come and pay their respects from afar; they are British and rock & roll straight from the American womb.

Elton came on the scene at the right moment at the beginning of the '70s and he has become very much part of the general revival of '50s music. When he first played the States and New York he went with cascading strings and cellos resounding from his American hit album, "Elton John". And they doubtless expected a rather poetic Elton. Yet he hit Americans most with some dazzling renditions of rock & roll and some would say that he even plays and sings better than one of his own heroes, Jerry Lee Lewis.

Whilst Elton reveres the music America produced he himself has brought a new dimension to the scene in which '50s music is either remembered or discarded. As Penny Valentine said in the music weekly *Sounds*, "Elton John took Vaudeville and funk to Los Angeles and in return they hailed him as Mr Rock and Roll."

The early American influences have lasted throughout his work and are verified by black American appreciation of his work amongst their own "funk" and the general American feeling that Elton is one of their own kind. Although Elton always insists Britain is his home, by the end of 1975 he was spending an increasing amount of time in the States. Certainly he would be justified in setting up home in America since there he receives open-armed acclamation whilst in Britain too many people stand like vultures waiting for dead flesh — though such individuals usually come from "hip" circles and some quarters of the musical press.

In basic human terms America and Elton feed off each other. He is an exhibitionist and America loves pageant, splendor and a degree of larger-than-life showmanship. At Anaheim Stadium, not far from Disneyland, Elton appeared for his 1972 concert in

Elton, seen from backstage, plays to a large crowd in the States.

Chris Walker

Above left: On American television, with Cher, Bette Midler and Flip Wilson. Below left: Made up as an old man for an American comedy TV show. Below centre: Playing with the Beachboys. Left: Elton on Soultrain. Above: A hug from Cher.

an Uncle Sam outfit, red, white, blue and silver colors permeating his garb and, perched on his head, a top hat in three colors. The audience loved it. Three years later in '75, he was at Dodger Stadium, L.A. and he wore the colors and adapted garb of the Dodgers team. Some of course would call Elton calculating. That may be true but most would maintain that the basic reason for Elton's "right" dress lies less in the overt currying of favor than in a genuine love for what is America and what he is, for a time, part of.

The pace of American city life, its diversity of cultures and lifestyle, its city tolerance of so-called deviants, becomes part of Elton's own system. He is supercharged and when he plays, concerts may last over three hours and are exhausting occasions both for him and the audience. The average rock star usually deigns to give only an hour or so of his music. Some Americans, during Elton's 1973 performances in New York, described him as a human power station — no mean compliment from people in a city as frantic and high as the East Coast location.

But then Elton has this great American crush. He doesn't yearn to be American. He's British. He just assimilates and loves much of Stateside music history and culture. And Americans love him — whereas it usually takes an artist six cross-country tours to establish himself, it took Elton just two.

Elton travels very frequently to and from Los Angeles. These recent pictures of the superstar show him arriving at and leaving from London's Heathrow airport, with Mrs June Bolan (top), and Connie Papras, his US co-manager (right).

Right: Solid gold Elton, covered with stars and badges, LA, late 1975.

LIFESTYLE AND SHOWMANSHIP

Few profess intimate knowledge of what makes Elton John tick. At best people can observe.

His forte in pop terms is an ability to turn upside down the conventional norms of what a pop star shall look like.

Elton does not meet the requirements of the good-looking pin-up male star whose physical features and winning smile will entice girls to buy his music, even if he cannot really sing or play his musical instrument with any inventiveness.

His physical statistics are definitely not attractive with the line-up reading 40-44-42. As a kid he says he was fat and shy and had a large inferiority complex. Even now, much later in life, he possesses outside of public gaze a certain sense of insecurity accompanied with a touching sensitivity.

Time has not improved his looks. *New Musical Express* writer Charles Murray once described him as someone with joke-face mask and a head

like a coconut. Murray said Elton's clothes defy all rules; everything, whether boots, pants, vest or shirt, even those famous braces he wears, is usually in conflict with everything else.

Yet people do not laugh at Elton John. Murray doesn't for one. Elton breaks all rules and wins through. For one thing he has an infectious air about him which makes the absurd seem reasonable, and for another he has an ability to play games in person and dress which many would, deep down, love to ape.

He obviously enjoys being a star and the quasi-psychologist might well say, and possibly be right, that he acts out the "only" child syndrome. He likes being at the center of attraction and at the same time can pander to his inner yearnings.

He takes delight in his music and with this comes, one feels, positive enjoyment at confronting the myriad hard-bitten, over-serious, intellectual exponents of rock music with something that loves and moves people to emotion. Elton audiences, as many have observed, have a religious air

Monitor

London Features International

Top pictures: Just four of the many pairs of glasses in Elton's enormous collection. Below: Elton's luxurious home.

Contrast: there's no limit to the range in Elton's wardrobe.

about them. There is deep commitment to the singer. They rise on their feet and greet songs and then sink back on their heels letting the sound waft over and through them. Unlike those of other performers they are rarely, if ever, rowdy.

Elton projects no sexual drive and his manager John Reid told journalists who accompanied Elton's many friends on his British Airways 707 jaunt to Los Angeles in October, 1975, that "Elton sometimes thinks of himself as the Cliff Richard of rock & roll. I think people see him as an amiable, very talented eccentric, which he is." John Reid said Elton has a fun image and he is not a star who goes around smashing up hotel rooms and added, "Many people can identify with him."

The songs Elton sings are of course sometimes more than just "fun" numbers. There is social protest and commentary, though not in the earthy manner, say, associated with the early Fugs or MC 5. There is neither the bitterness of early Dylan nor the sweetness amidst the telling points of Joan Baez. Mike Flood Page and Chris Salewicz perhaps arrive at the nitty gritty by saying in *Let It Rock* (September, 1973), "his songs with political and social comment are set in contexts so far in time and space from our everyday lives as to remove any power to challenge. At most they demand no more than sympathy for the underdog."

And this certainly does not suggest that there lurks in Elton a selfish, corrupt, cynical manipulator. Far from it. He lives, breathes and believes in his music and he has never compromised. Those who dislike what he does do so more because he does not fit into their categories than for any other reason. After all, in rock there exists amongst

73

devotees a curious, though psychologically meaningful, desire to preserve certain kinds of music and artists as theirs. Elton like Simon and Garfunkel, certainly Paul McCartney, and even to some extent, via "Imagine", John Lennon can make sense to a variety of musical groups.

Fame has brought him money which he has used generously. He is good to his friends. Not many pop stars would buy their manager a yacht for his birthday and a ring worth a few thousand pounds. Elton says his royal giving comes from a basic pragmatic philosophy which says quite simply that he could be run over by a bus in a few hours' time, so why not enjoy things and people, now.

In conversation he will associate his present life-style with a withdrawn childhood and say, "So now, I'm just making up for lost time and I'm having a ball doing it." The ball is more than clothes, it extends to his concerts which are rarely straight, predictable affairs. They are big birthday parties.

And so Elton John with music, color and excitement has become one of the most successful artists of the '70s and arguably the world's biggest draw at the time of writing.

Along the way he has attracted thousands, millions, of fans but has also suffered from unpleasant experiences and people. He told Penny Valentine in 1971, "I've gone out of my way to be nice to everyone and I end up getting kicked in the teeth for it".

But he knows in the end that he wins. It's when no one complains, no one carps, that there is real cause to worry. Since he is so often surrounded by adoring thousands, and his concerts sell out in hours, why should he bother? He is a truly great star.

Dogs are used as a motif on this jacket (below), and greet him and his mother (right) by the pool.

Ian Vaughan/Transworld

S.K.R.

RECORDS
AND RECORDING

BEHIND THE ALBUMS

Terry O'Neill

empty sky / elton john

The first Elton John album, "Empty Sky," was made in a four-track studio at DJM records. Elton remembers above all the electric piano hired for the occasion. It was out of tune, which meant that he had to play round many of the notes. Elton was not impressed by the recording but apparently became partial to it after its favorable reception by BBC producers and the general record-buying public. The album sold more than a reasonable 20,000 copies. It gave Elton and Bernie Taupin the confidence to continue. Previous to this, several recording projects had failed completely. These included Elton recording under producer Zack Laurence and his attempt to record a Mark London song entitled "Best Of Both Worlds".

The second album, "Elton John", was much more sophisticated. Steve Brown, the producer of "Empty Sky", felt that a different producer should be

utilized. At the same time need was felt for someone to arrange the kind of material Bernie and Elton were producing at this time, as it was suitable for orchestration. They therefore approached ex-Beatles producer and arranger, George Martin, but he declined. Several other blanks were drawn and the duo were in despair. However, on the advice of ace record-plugger, Tony Hall, they went to see Paul Buckmaster, who had been the arranger for Arrival and hit disc, "Friends".

Buckmaster heard "Your Song" and then other songs from Elton-Bernie tapes and was impressed. He agreed to work with them and suggested they ask Gus Dudgeon to produce the album. At first Dudgeon was not forthcoming, but eventually he said yes. The album was made live and cost £6500 ($16,000). Orchestration was planned track by track with careful sketching of which instruments would play on particular tracks. Album tracks were cut and in addition "Grey Seal" (later the B side of "Rock & Roll Madonna"), "In The Old Man's Shoes", and another future B side, "Bad Side Of The Moon" (which became the reverse of "Border Song").

The song which had most impact was "Border Song", and when it was released as a single in March, 1970, it led to Elton's first appearance on the BBC TV programme, Top Of The Pops. The album, "Elton John", came out two months later and, doubtless helped by the single's minor success, reached no. 45 in the music trade papers' chart and sold 4,000 copies in the first couple of weeks.

However, initial reaction was no guide and the album was seen by the

Elton John

team as a disappointing event. Elton later felt the album misled a number of people whereas "Empty Sky" represented better the true essence of the group. He saw "Empty Sky" as possessing Stones' influence, whilst "Elton John" marked the beginning of a romantic image to be associated with his music. Elton told the British musical paper, *New Musical Express*, in February, 1975, "If the cover for the 'Elton John' album hadn't been so mean and moody it wouldn't have been so bad, but everyone thought I was going to come out on stage and be very sensitive like Peter Skellern."

The album "Elton John" did, however, lead Elton across the Atlantic and, with Nigel Olsson and bassman Dee Murray, he played in the States for three weeks. Olsson had come via Plastic Penny and one of the many Spencer Davis groups. Murray had been with Mirage and then with the same Spencer Davis line-up as Olsson. As a trio they existed from April, 1970, to January, 1972, and so were involved in future album recording. America made Elton and his team instant stars and the "Elton John" disc soon made the US Top 20. After such success, in contrast with early British response, there was no question of not continuing with further albums.

The third album, "Tumbleweed Connection", came from common material available at the time of "Elton John", and features one of Elton's favorite record sleeves by designer and artist, David Larkham. "Tumbleweed" was issued whilst "Elton John" was still in the US Top Ten and soon both were fighting a battle for highest position. When Elton returned from the States both "Elton John" and "Tumbleweed Connection" became hits in Britain.

Elton's next two albums, "Friends" and "17-11-70", were described by the British rock magazine, *Let It Rock*, as a "swift slide into mediocrity". "Friends" was issued in April, 1971, and comprised the score of the film *Friends*, written by Elton and Bernie.

Richie Havens had been approached by the film company but with his refusal they turned toward the Taupin-John team. The film disappeared without trace and the music album itself was soon laid to rest and only resurrected later by rock musicologists and historians.

The album was made in four weeks. After an abortive recording at Olympic studios, London, it was re-recorded at Trident Studios, also in London. It contained several additional songs as extras to the soundtrack, partly because Elton couldn't stomach the conventional film-score disc which contained minutes of sound extraneous to the actual music. Thus he added songs which had been saved for the "Tumbleweed" album but not used. These were "Honky Roll" and "Can I Put You On?"

The "Friends" film-score effort has been Elton's only attempt at complete score writing; even though it was

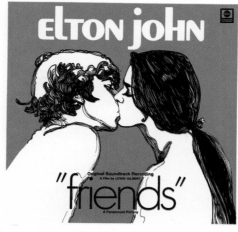

somewhat abortive, it did teach him and Paul Buckmaster something of the nature of this musical writing art. It also came at a time when he was rather depressed and feeling that his musical magic was departing. Buckmaster was experiencing similar feelings and he told *Sounds*, the British music weekly, that he would sit for hours listening to music by other people, like Stockhausen and Bach, rather than get down to writing the necessary film score. He told the paper's writer, Penny Valentine, "There are times when I've got out the paper and just found myself staring at it for about four hours and freaking out in panic . . . I have these horrible paranoias about losing what I've got as a musician."

"17-11-70" had the same release month as "Friends" and was a live album. Whilst touring the States Elton was asked to do a live performance for the New York station, WABC. It would be a studio recording and broadcast in stereo. An audience of around a hundred people helped in the creation of a good atmosphere.

Elton was quite unaware that the studio concert was not only broadcast but being recorded on an eight-track machine. When he and the others listened to the recording there was a favorable response and Elton was particularly encouraged by the prominent part on the recording played by Dee Murray and Nigel Olsson.

With the imminent release of the disappointing *Friends* material the decision was made to issue the New York radio station concert recording as an album. At DJM studios in London a quick mix was made and consequently "17-11-70", the concert's date, was penciled in for release.

Apparently Elton thinks little of the album but the American release gave him his fourth album in the US Top 30, a feat previously achieved only by the Beatles. Its sales figure of under 350,000 was disappointing, however, and was probably due to the fact that American radio stations gave it extensive air coverage prior to release and doubtless many people taped the material; others bought imported copies from Britain. A different mix was made for the American album release and Elton has said this is preferable to the British copy.

Elton's next studio album, "Madman Across The Water", fell, according to *Let It Rock*, into the same category as the "Friends" and "17-11-70" discs and they told their readers, "Opinions differ as to which is the real dregs."

It was released in October, 1971, and for some people this became a disaster year for Elton. Whatever the critical response toward the three albums it had no measurable effect upon the kind of concert attendances Elton enjoyed in the States. His concerts were sell-outs.

"Madman Across The Water" was for various reasons seen at the time as being the last orchestrated album. There was the long-standing rock & roll love in Elton's musical system and a desire to free himself from the kind of image orchestration had built up in many people's minds. He also saw imminent change being occasioned by his signing of a guitarist to his band, in the person of Davey Johnstone. In addition, Paul Buckmaster, the musical arranger, said he wanted to pursue his talents in other directions and so "Madman Across The Water" represented the closing of an Elton John recording era. The disc did have one major memory for writer Bernie Taupin. Bernie had bought a cottage in his native Lincolnshire and married a girl called Maxine whom he had met in America. "Tiny Dancer" on the album is a song about her.

"Honky Chateau" came next and featured a bearded Elton on the record sleeve. It was recorded at the Strawberry Studios in France, and re-mixed at Trident in London.

With the addition of Davey Johnstone there was the opportunity for the guitar to take over many of the tune lines and so leave Elton with freedom to embellish. Interestingly enough when Davey was signed to the Band it was purely on account of his acoustic work for the group Magna Carta-but Elton saw him as a future great electric guitarist.

"Honky Chateau" was the Band's first no. 1 album in America and in Britain it helped to counteract much of the 1971 criticism. The following album, "Don't Shoot Me, I'm Only The Piano Player", was also recorded in France but at a different time. It saw Paul Buckmaster return with some orchestral arrangements, but nevertheless the rock & roll feel on the disc was retained. The engineer credited on the album sleeve was Ken Scott who, in 1975, achieved renown for his work with "Supertramp".

Elton, at this time feeling pretty the worse for wear and on the verge of a mental breakdown, had arranged for a month's vacation in Los Angeles. However, he persuaded himself it might be a good idea to lay down one track and then continue with the remainder when he returned from his vacation.

Work commenced on "Daniel", the song after which Rob Townshend, *ex-Family and Medicine Head* and his wife, Caroline, named their first son. However, more than one track was laid, and though Elton says he felt "down" during the making of this

album, amazingly enough the final sound was anything but this.

The first side was later called by Elton his "discotheque album" and one other feature of some interest was a song on side two called "I'm Going To Be A Teenage Idol", a number which was dedicated to Marc Bolan, who apparently enjoyed it.

For Elton the disc was a vital moment in his career. He told *Zig Zag*'s John Tobler, "It was either giving up, or using the band on record. When we got Davey in, it's just gone from then. I could never go back to using session musicians again as such, because it's so much better now."

A double record album followed and this disc, "Goodbye Yellow Brick Road", with its myriad musical styles, often provocative lyrics, and, when utilized, imaginative musical scoring, satisfied most critics. Elton was riding high once more.

The album was more or less without blemish and will doubtless become one of the great albums of the '70s. It had an amazing consistency spread over its 20 tracks. As usual DJM took tracks from the album and released them as singles. This particular album produced three hits. One of them, "Saturday Night's Alright For Fighting", was released in June, 1973 and acted as a powerful trailer for the album itself which was released in October.

America went for "Bennie And The Jets", a track from the album which was only a B-side in Britain. This pulsating, strongly rhythmic number even captured very strong interest from black music stations, and Elton became one of the very few white artists ever to have made the soul-chart listings.

Although this article is specifically concerned with albums, mention should be made of the single, "Step Into Christmas". Elton has recorded very few songs specifically for single release, and usually his singles have been prominent and successful trailers for album offerings, prior to inclusion

on the respective albums. So why did Elton issue and especially record a seasonal song? Elton called it "a real loon about and something we'd like to do a lot more of".

The song was written on a Saturday morning, recorded later in the day and issued less than a week later. Bernie Taupin's lyrics give further reason for they expressed a "thank-you" to everybody for making 1973 such a productive and artistically satisfying year. The record's B side expressed the loony feel in no uncertain terms, the title being "Ho Ho — Who'd Be A Turkey At Christmas?" Of his vocal performance on this track, Elton said, "As a matter of fact I sound a bit like the Ronettes on it."

For some music critics, "Yellow Brick Road" reached an Elton peak and they say since its issue, both singer

and songwriter have been finding their way back down a slope towards the mediocrity of 1971. Others might concede that albums since have not been of similar standard but would argue that by and large his records have been satisfactory and certainly far better than the general run of released material on British and American markets. Whatever may or may not be the truth of these opinions, the now statutory sell-out of Elton John has been quite unaffected.

"Caribou" saw new band member Ray Cooper now firmly entrenched in the group, though Cooper had played on various "Yellow Brick Road" cuts. Two album cuts became single hits, "The Bitch Is Back" and "Don't Let The Sun Go Down", the latter being one of Elton's biggest single sellers. Interestingly, "The Bitch Is Back" was the only E.J. title on the large juke-box selection at his 1974 hired house in the L.A. area of Beverly Hills. And be that as it may, "Caribou" has usually received from Elton's own lips less praise than knocking. "Goodbye Yellow Brick Road" has had its problems, particularly because of Elton's ill-fated Jamaican venture, yet the final result was good. "Caribou" had its quota of

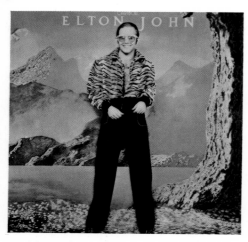

problems but these were never really eradicated.

Elton was in the middle of another of his traumatic periods of declining health due to the rigors of his usual work and music commitments. Time was in any case short with tours of Japan and Australia planned and with nothing really in the can. "Caribou" was recorded in some haste, 10 days in all, though two of these were lost because of studio mechanical problems. For some people "Don't Let The Sun Go Down" has become a classic number, yet for Elton its recording was a nightmare. He told Britain's *New Musical Express*, "I thought it was the worst vocal of all time, and I said: 'I hate it. I hate my vocals so don't you dare put this on the album.'" Elton was nominated for an Oscar under the Grammy Awards Best Vocal Performance.

"Caribou", a June release, was Elton's only offering in 1974 and indeed no new product came until May of 1975 when, in lavish style, came "Captain Fantastic and the Brown Dirt Cowboy".

In between the two albums DJM did release the first of a series of Elton's greatest trackings, under the unadventurous title of "Elton John's Greatest Hits". More cheering at the time, however, was another brand-new single recording, namely, "Lucy In The Sky With Diamonds". Elton had met John Lennon and thoroughly enjoyed his company. In recording terms it meant both lending a hand on respective disc adventures. The single was deservedly a hit.

"Captain Fantastic" came packaged, the packaging comprising several booklets enclosed with the disc, one of which gave cuttings and photographs of early days, the other, lyrics of this particular disc. The front and back covers of this album depicted the record's intent — an autobiographical work which was aimed on capturing the duo's early musical struggles.

Sounds writer, Penny Valentine wrote, "For once Elton is singing about himself and not simply giving voice to images and emotions which ostensibly are drawn from Bernie's experience alone. Just as Elton was more exposed than ever in New York in the studio (at the NY preview) so he is more exposed than ever on this album." She saw "that hint of danger" bringing out positive musical adventures from Elton which had been missing from more recent albums.

Elton called the disc, "very open and honest" and thought the very fact that he could relate personally to the words had improved his vocal interpretation. For once, he had produced an album without immediate commercial appeal and without songs that instantly lent themselves to successful single release. In Britain and in America, DJM and MCA respectively, issued "Someone Saved My Life Tonight". The song, with its Elton autobiographical touches, had most success in America.

There were good words spoken about "Captain Fantastic", in the vein and spirit of Penny Valentine, but accolades were not exactly in abundance.

The October, 1975, issue of "Rock Of The Westies" saw changes in the Elton John Band personnel. Gone were Nigel Olsson and Dee Murray and plans to enlarge the band from a five-piece set-up had been materialized with seven musicians plus Elton credited on the sleeve.

One interesting new member is Caleb Quaye, though Elton connoisseurs will know his name from almost the beginning of Elton's musical days. Quaye was part of Bluesology 5 and played guitar plus working at DJM studios. He was also in part responsible for the early Elton demos and later played on "Empty Sky". Another extremely interesting addition was Roger Pope on drums. He, too, had played on "Empty Sky" and in early days had been with the Soul Agents, the Loot and with Hookfoot during several changes of personnel.

"Rock Of The Westies" went straight to the top of Billboard's Top 200 albums, the second time Elton had achieved such a feat, whilst he also hit no. 1 in the American singles chart with the catchy "Island Girl". Britain allowed the album into the Top 5 but decided against the single just as it seemed destined for the Top 10.

Again it must be said that there was a certain lukewarmness amongst the musical writing fraternity at this Elton offering. But whatever the reaction of this group, the business fraternity of the record world could see another high-selling Elton album.

With "Rock Of The Westies" Elton reached the last but one album of his recording contract with DJM, a relationship which goes back to his very first album and indeed single as a solo artist; his initial records were leased by DJM to Phonogram, because DJM had not established itself as a record company.

The one remaining disc is another compilation hit album. And how long Elton continues as a recording artist or as part of a band remains an open question. On several occasions Elton John has threatened his retirement. Whatever may be the outcome, from the vantage point of the mid-'70s it can be said that Elton John and his various bands have been one of the best-selling sounds in contemporary music.

THE ROCKET LABEL

For many years Elton must have entertained thoughts of being his own boss and running his own record company, even though through sheer practical necessity various operational powers would lie in the hands of others.

Reality became sharply divorced from daydreams and the first steps were taken in the formation of a company when Elton and manager John Reid discussed with Steve Brown the inability to find good recording terms for band member Davey Johnstone. The trio saw the formation of their record company as the obvious answer. The idea became more than mere idle talk and Elton came up with the proposed company name, Rocket Records.

The name was good and an engaging logo was chosen of a smiling face at the front of a railway engine with carriages and friendly occupants trailing behind. It took six months of hard planning for various business decisions to be made and for the Rocket Records headquarters to be established in London's famous Wardour Street. There they stayed from the company's inception in 1970 until the fall of 1975 when the move was made to a location in the vicinity of the American Embassy, London.

At the time of the company's formation Elton talked expansively and with some grandeur of its purpose. Money was important but considered as secondary to artistic integrity and the issuing of good-quality product. Hopefully the company would find either brand-new talent or someone on the brink of success just waiting for the right guidance and direction. The former hope was realized in a record contract for a Welsh schoolboy called Maldwyn Pope and the latter in the breakthrough of Kiki Dee in Britain and in the resurgence of stardom for a name-selling artist of the '50s, Neil Sedaka, in the States.

Elton saw Rocket Records as a company with a small roster, thus a moderate release schedule, and with time to cultivate a family atmosphere and more-than-usual care of signed artists. Eventually he expected his own name would appear on the label.

Rocket would be geared towards listening to and hearing unknown artists, and because of this he was

London Features International

Stars of the Rocket Record Company: Elton with Kiki Dee (above) and celebrating with Neil Sedaka and Bernie (left).

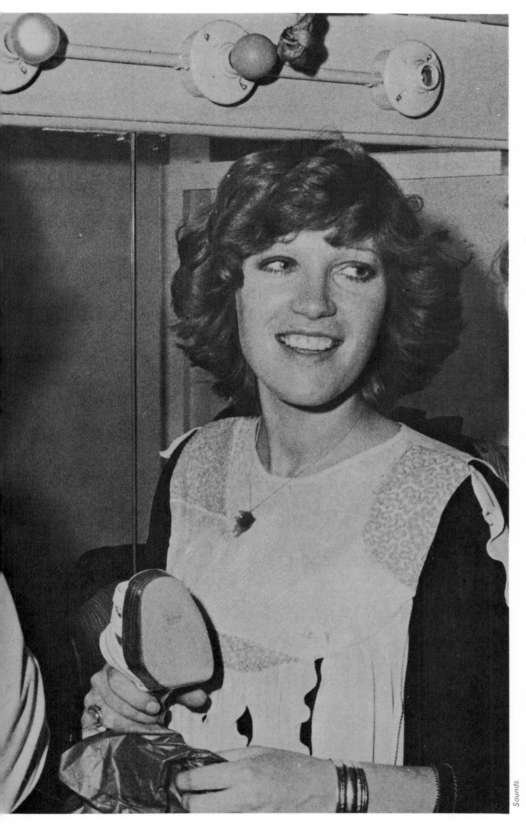
Sounds.

disaster, though he could foresee its growth and the problems this could cause in relation to his general philosophy.

The label's first British chart hit came from Kiki Dee. Kiki had recorded elsewhere for some time and been constantly on the verge of major success. She had backed many a famous name including Dusty Springfield. In spite of the general agreement within the industry that she had talent, she had never savored fame.

With Rocket it happened and her disc of "Amoureuse" made the British Top 20. It was a hit for the company's fourth single. At the time, Elton said that his previous ambition for a family atmosphere in the company had become reality. When Kiki sang at a gig near London all the record company personnel went. He told how he rang up every day for Kiki's sale figures, which would give indication of possible chart position by the next published listings.

Kiki Dee made the charts with a ballad, but basically Rocket saw her forte lying in more raunchy, rock-styled numbers. They hoped the hit "Amoureuse" would make her name more familiar and enable her other material to find a listening audience. Their hopes were rewarded when "I Got The Music In Me" became a big hit. Elton told the *New Musical Express*, "All we've done is given her the confidence to do it on her own. And there's so many people in the business like me who can do these things for artists like Kiki Dee".

In America he brought Neil Sedaka back into prominence. On Rocket, Sedaka has become a major song-writer of the '70s, and not merely a resurrected rock & roll figure from the late '50s and early '60s, via numbers like "I Go Ape" and "Breaking Up Is Hard To Do", songs contrasting vividly in style with the 1975 hit, "The Immigrant", or the pathos and tenderness of "Solitude".

Several Elton John Band members have had solo material released on the label, notably Davey Johnstone and Nigel Olsson. Olsson sings rather than drums his way to the fore and has enjoyed continental success and hit-parade fortunes in Scandinavia.

In 1975 Elton John and his business team moved from Island distribution into the massive kingdom of EMI and Elton himself was no longer an artist with a DJM future. For Rocket, like Elton, a new future was being created and news began filtering through of another Rocket experiment. This was the reported attempt at making Cliff Richard, a major British artist since 1959 with more hits than any other artist or group, at long last a name for Americans to conjure with.

Obviously Rocket does not stand still on its tracks.

pleased his own record product was not on Rocket for this would detract from the interest in less known artists, those who in time could become stars.

Elton saw his operation as a form of protest against the massive companies with all their controlling interests. He would encourage variety and his label would not automatically mean a certain kind of approach. He told the musical paper, *Melody Maker*, "Although I like Asylum for example, everyone on Asylum is in the same bag. You put the record on and you know you're going to hear acoustic songs and close harmonies."

What he did not see was Rocket expanding in a form similar or equivalent to that of the once idealistic Apple company, which ended in

THE MUSICIANS

Terry O'Neill

NIGEL OLSSON

Nigel Olsson was born in Cheshire, England, on February 10, 1949. At St. Chad's boarding school in North Wales he became interested in the skiffle music of Lonnie ("Rock Island Line") Donnegan and bought an acoustic guitar. The family moved to Sunderland in the north-east when Nigel was 13. He went to Hilton Redhouse Comprehensive School where his studies included seamanship, and while he was there he played with local groups.

Nigel worked as an electrician and car mechanic while playing semi-professionally with a group called Fallout, who were strongly influenced by Memphis Sim. It was here that he started to play the drums.

Nigel made his professional bow with Plastic Penny in December 1967, and the group topped the British charts soon afterwards with "Everything I Am". Plastic Penny split in 1968 and some weeks later he joined his friend Dee Murray in the Spencer Davis Group. Nigel and Dee had known and admired Elton before they joined him some months after leaving Davis.

Like Dee, Nigel remembers wondering how much could be done with just piano, bass and drums. There were initial problems with the amplification of the piano but these were solved after Nigel had bought a new drum kit.

Nigel left the Band in 1975 to pursue a solo career. He recorded an album "The Drum, Orchestra and Chorus" in 1971; some time later a single "Only One Woman" was made on the Rocket label. These two discs have been followed by a single "Something Lacking In Me" and an album entitled "Nigel Olsson", both on the Rocket label.

KENNY PASSARELLI

Terry O'Neill

Kenny, the fretless bass and background vocals member of the Elton John Band, has played with Joe Walsh's Barnstorm and Stephen Stills' Manassas. He comes from Denver, Colorado, and there played with various high-school bands. He did session work prior to joining Joe Walsh and Barnstorm. When that group split he moved into Manassas and whilst with this outfit found time to help out on albums from Dan Fogelberg and Veronique Sanson. On leaving Manassas he joined with ex-Barnstormer Joe Vitale for a US East Coast tour.

While in New York a call from Joe Walsh told him he had been recommended to the Elton John Band and when Elton himself called and invited him to join, Kenny Passarelli flew off to Paris where the Band were located.

One interesting sideline on Kenny Passarelli is his having spent 18 years studying classical trumpet.

DEE MURRAY

Bassman Dee Murray was born in Kent, England, on April 3, 1946. His

Terry O'Neill

real name is David Murray Oates. The family moved to Southgate, North London, in 1953 and Dee went to Ashmole Secondary Modern School. He had a couple of piano lessons when young and then taught himself. At 16, he started work in the stores department of a car firm.

He used his first earnings to buy a player and discs. He played with a group called Mirage for three years and wrote a few songs. Then, in the autumn of 1968 he joined the Spencer Davis group and toured the States with them, but he left in the spring of 1969 and joined Elton John shortly afterwards. He and Nigel Olsson had gained valuable experience during their few months together with Davis. Dee was a member of the Elton John Band until late 1975.

Dee's home is a detached house in North London, where he lives with his wife Anett. His proudest possession is his ultra-modern sound system.

RAY COOPER

Ray began in the world of classical music and studied classical piano for 12 years before acquiring a love for wind and string instruments. Ray, who was born in Hertfordshire, has mastered endless percussion sounds and besides being involved in rock has had a jazz background. In the latter he has played with Maynard Ferguson, John Dankworth, and Cleo Laine. In the world of rock & roll he has played on session work with a star-studded list of The Rolling Stones, various ex-

Terry O'Neill

Beatles, Harry Nilsson, Carly Simon, America, and others. Like Davey Johnstone he came into contact with Elton through session work and after some involvement with Blue Mink Ray joined Elton's Band in 1973, stepping onto a stage at Liverpool without a moment's rehearsal. Fortunately, he knew the material since he had played on every Elton album except "Empty Sky".

Terry O'Neill

JAMES NEWTON-HOWARD

Howard is the electronic keyboards and synthesizer member of the Elton John Band. His association with rock & roll has been brief, dating from the beginning of the '70s. He has played with a wealth of talent and has been listed as a musician on albums from Carly Simon, Ringo Starr, and Art Garfunkel. He was born and bred in Los Angeles and studied classical piano.

On leaving music college he played in a number of bands and thence into studio work. An album titled after his own name was issued in 1974. On the basis of that and his recording work Elton hired him for the Band. There was no audition.

Terry O'Neill

CALEB QUAY

Caleb met Elton when both were music-publishing employees. Several years after meeting they joined forces with Bluesology at the time when the band were backing Long John Baldry.

Caleb had been playing musical instruments from an early age and by the time he was 16 had become staff-musician-producer-engineer in Dick James's gargantuan publishing operation, and was producing demos for everyone from Troggs to the Hollies. Caleb produced Elton's first-ever single and "thirty tracks" for an album which was never issued. Quaye was one of the co-founder members of Hookfoot but always remained close to Elton and played on "Empty Sky", "Elton John", "Tumbleweed Connection", and "Madman Across The Water". When Hookfoot ceased operation he left for Chicago and played session work until Elton John invited him to join the Band.

ROGER POPE

Roger Pope is English and was born at Whitstable, Kent. He was once a member of Soul Agent and was there for four years including a six-month period when Rod Stewart was lead vocalist.

After the group split, Roger met up with Caleb Quaye and Dave Glover, and through Quaye, Elton John. Roger was the drummer on Elton's first single,

Terry O'Neill

"Lady Samantha", and his initial album, "Empty Sky". Out of Elton's sessions came Hookfoot and the band lasted five years during which time four albums and a number of singles were issued. Roger Pope still found time to play on the "Tumbleweed Connection" and "Madman Across The Water" albums. When Hookfoot broke up early in 1974, Roger joined the Kiki Dee Band for the mammoth American tour of that summer. Shortly afterwards he became the drummer in the new Elton John Band.

Terry O'Neill

BERNIE TAUPIN

Bernie Taupin is an integral part of the Elton John phenomenon and has been a prolific writer. His meeting with Elton and subsequent musical adventures are described elsewhere in this volume but Bernie has been broadening his activities. He has had a book published, *The One Who Writes The*

Words, which is basically a book of his lyrics with illustrations by Alan Aldridge, and a handful of drawings by rock-celebrities thrown in.

He has also become a record producer and in 1975 he produced the Hudson Brothers' disc, "Rendezvous", a success in America, though not in Britain.

DAVEY JOHNSTONE

Ever since "Madman Across The Water", Davey has become an important part of Elton's music and he became a permanent member of the Elton John Band with the recording of "Honky Chateau". Davey was born in Edinburgh on May 6th, 1951, and began playing the violin at the age of seven. Like Caleb Quaye, he picked up the guitar at 12 and by the time he was sixteen had taught himself banjo and mandolin. He was faced at this point in his life with a choice between art college and music. He chose the latter and found his first footing in the folk-music world. He became a member of Noel Murphy's Draught Porridge. To those who heard his musical ability it was obvious he was destined for great things but prior to joining the Elton John world he became a member of Magna Carta. He did some session work and there came into contact with Elton's producer, Gus Dudgeon, and this led on to playing on the "Madman" sessions. Then, of course, came the permanent arrangement with Elton. Davey has one child and he makes reference to his son in the title of his first solo album, "Smiling Face". 1976 sees the release of his second L.P. He played on Bernie Taupin's album, "Taupin", and on Nigel Olsson's single, "Only One Woman". Some of his songs are featured on his first album under the Rocket logo.

86

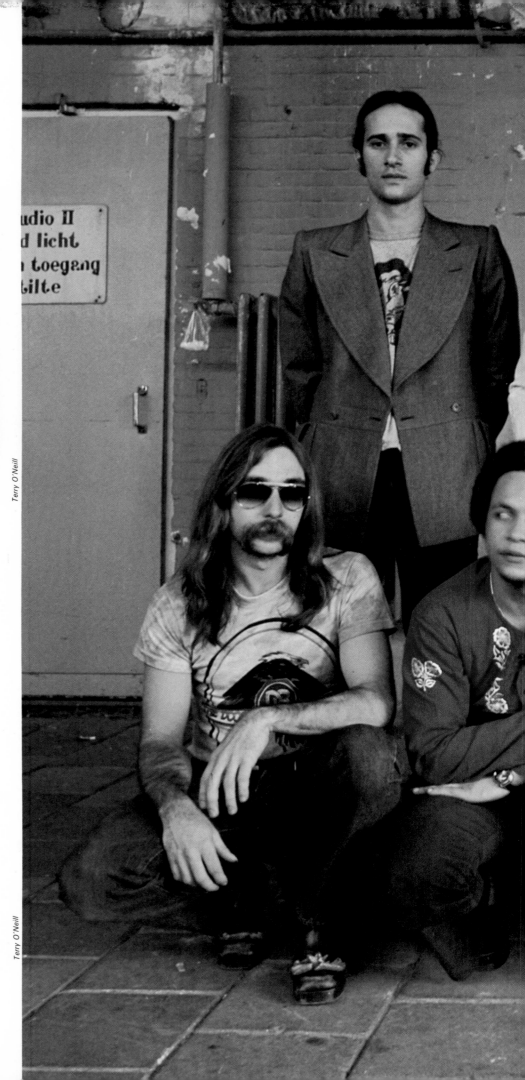

Terry O'Neill

Terry O'Neill

ELTON'S DIARY

1947 In Pinner, Middlesex, England, Sheila, wife of Stanley, Dwight gives birth to a son and calls him Reginald Kenneth. He is an only child.

1951 Reginald has his first piano lessons.

1958 He passes 11-plus examination and so attends Pinner County Grammar School.

1959 He plays at the Ruislip-Norwood Music Festival, Middlesex.

1964/5 Leaves school and obtains a tea-boy job with Mills Music. He also packs parcels and delivers internal post.

1964/5 Plays piano at weekends for the proprietor of the North-wood Hills Hotel for £1 ($2.50) per evening.

1964/5 Joins up with a local semi-pro group in the Harrow area called Bluesology. He plays organ.

1965 Bluesology, still semi-pro, make recordings for Fontana records. Two discs are "Come Back Baby" and "Mr Frantic". Elton, still as Reg Dwight, sings lead vocal on the first and not the group's main singer, Stuart Brown. Both discs are released and lost.

1966/7 Elton leaves Mills. Bluesology audition on a Saturday morning at Kilburn State and sign with the Roy Tempest Agency. They back American soul bands and singers. The band is now professional. It leaves the Tempest Agency and signs with Marquee Artists. Bluesology go through personnel changes, their third upheaval. They meet and join forces with Long John Baldry. Baldry takes over and has two hits. At this stage the band reforms and among new members are Marsha Hunt and Neil Hubbard; both stay only a short while.

1967 Elton auditions as a singer for Liberty Records but fails. He meets Bernie Taupin. First Dwight-Taupin songs are published. They sign with DJM publishing and Elton also signs as a singer. Bluesology still continue.

1968 Bluesology record for Polydor and disc called "Since I Met You Baby" is produced by Kenny Lynch. Elton's record "I've Been Loving You" is released by Philips. Elton changes his name from Reg Dwight to Elton John. He plays last gig with Baldry and Bluesology. A Taupin-John song,

"I Can't Go On Living Without You", reaches last six considered songs for Eurovision Song Contest. It is later recorded by Cilla Black. Another of their songs, "The Tide Will Turn For Rebecca", is recorded by Edward Woodward. Elton meets Steve Brown and Brown becomes his producer for a time.

1969 Philips release "Lady Samantha" with "All Across

The Heavens'' as the B side. DJM start their own label and issue in May, 1969, ''It's Me That You Need.'' First album is issued: ''Empty Sky''. BBC give it considerable airplay.

1970 The ''Elton John'' album released. It enters Music Week charts at 45 but then hurriedly departs. Also in 1970, ''Tumbleweed Connection''. Material for both culled from a stockpile of songs large enough to provide material for three albums. Several songs on the ''Elton John'' album get recorded by other people, particularly, ''Pilot'', ''Border Song'' and ''Sixty Years On''. Aretha Franklin records ''Border Song''. Elton forms a band, tours the States and meets with amazing success, particularly on the East Coast. His albums sell.

1971 He produces, with Rod Stewart, recording sessions with Long John Baldry in New York. With Bernie he writes for the film ''Friends'' and the disc is issued on Paramount records. Another album is released in April entitled ''17-11-70'', a ''live'' album. It was recorded on an eight-track tape recorder. British copy inferior to the Stateside issue which has a better mix. October sees issue of ''Madman Across The Water''. 1971 also saw British acclaim at long last. Elton begins a process of stunning people by his clothes. By now he has four hit US albums.

1972 He records ''Honky Chateau'' and ''Don't Shoot Me, I'm Only The Piano Player'' in France. Prior to leaving, Elton signed Davey Johnstone and with new emphasis upon guitar a greater rock & roll influence entered the record scene. More successful tours were enjoyed.

1973 ''Don't Shoot Me, I'm Only The Piano Player'' is a no. 1 hit in both British and US charts. Elton records ''Goodbye Yellow Brick Road'', a double album, which also tops both album charts. His late summer tour of America breaks all past attendance records established by Elvis

Presley and The Rolling Stones. Forms Rocket Records, though his own personal contract remains with DJM until 1976. The label has its first hit with ''Amoureuse'' from Kiki Dee. During December British TV shows Bryan Forbe's documentary on Elton's life-style. Elton holds five days of Christmas extravaganza at London's Hammersmith Odeon.

1974 The album ''Caribou'' is released; also one entitled ''Elton John's Greatest Hits''. Elton signs contract with MCA Records said to be worth $8,000,000 and enjoys a successful American tour. After touring Japan (where the ''Caribou'' album was finished), Australia and New Zealand, the band is exhausted and almost breaks up. April-May tour of Britain cancelled. In June the Band sails for the States in the SS *France*. Elton is invited by John Lennon to share his ''Walls and Bridges'' album and Lennon later joins the Band for the second ''Caribou'' recording. The new album is ''Captain Fantastic And The Brown Dirt Cowboy'' (not released until 1975). Elton records the Beatles hit, ''Lucy In The Sky With Diamonds'', with Lennon's aid. In Britain, Rocket achieves success with Kiki Dee's ''I Got The Music In Me''. Elton signs Neil Sedaka for Rocket in America and the veteran rock & roll singer and ace songwriter begins record hit life all over again.

1975 ''Captain Fantastic'' is released in May and followed the hit single ''Philadelphia Freedom''. The album is autobiographical. British reviews are lukewarm. Elton announces he will not sign a renewed contract with DJM and signs with EMI taking the Rocket Record company with him. In late October Elton transports 100 people from Britain to Los Angeles in order to see and hear his Dodger Stadium concert. The album, ''Rock Of The Westies'', is issued late October. British reviews off-hand but album goes straight to no. 5 and in America straight to no. 1, only the second time this has occurred in Billboards Top 200. (Elton was also the first to achieve this feat.) 1975 ends with one Elton album outstanding for DJM: this will contain live recordings made in recent years including Madison Square Gardens, New York and

the Wembley concert, London. (There may also be other compilation albums released by DJM in the future.) The year also saw personnel change in the Elton John Band, when Dee and Nigel left, and Roger Pope, James Newton-Howard, Caleb Quaye and Kenny Passarelli joined.

1976 The US trade paper *Billboard* reported, in its issue of January 17, 1976, that ''Elton John's Greatest Hits'' album, released in 1974, had been the first ever package of singles to hit the top of the US charts. On January 22 Elton accompanied Princess Margaret to a performance of the film, ''The Sunshine Boys''.

DISCOGRAPHY

SINGLES *

WITH BLUESOLOGY

Come Back Baby	July 1965
Mr Frantic	February 1966
Since I Met You Baby	1968

SINGLES BY ELTON JOHN*

I've Been Loving You	March 1968
Lady Samantha	January 1969
It's Me That You Need	May 1969
Border Song	March 1970
Rock And Roll Madonna	June 1970
Your Song	January 1971
Friends	April 1971
Rocket Man	April 1972
Honky Cat	August 1972
Crocodile Rock	October 1972
Daniel	January 1973
Saturday Night's Alright For Fighting	June 1973
Goodbye Yellow Brick Road	September 1973
Step Into Christmas	November 1973
Candle In The Wind	February 1974
Bennie And The Jets (U.S. only)	January 1974
Don't Let The Sun Go Down On Me	May 1974
The Bitch Is Back	August 1974
Lucy In The Sky With Diamonds	November 1974
Philadelphia Freedom	February 1975
Someone Saved My Life Tonight	June 1975
Island Girl	October 1975
Grow Some Funk Of Your Own	January 1976

ALBUMS *

Empty Sky	June 1969
Elton John	April 1970
Tumbleweed Connection	October 1970
17.11.70	April 1971
Madman Across The Water	October 1971
Honky Chateau	May 1972
Don't Shoot Me, I'm Only The Piano Player	January 1973
Goodbye Yellow Brick Road (Double Album)	October 1973
Caribou	June 1973
Elton John's Greatest Hits	November 1974
Captain Fantastic And The Brown Dirt Cowboy	May 1975
Rock Of The Westies	October 1975

FILM SCORE*

Friends	April 1971

*Not all discs had joint UK/US release.